THE BODY OF CHRIST.

THE BODY OF CHRIST

AN ENQUIRY INTO THE INSTITUTION AND
DOCTRINE OF HOLY COMMUNION

BY CHARLES GORE, M.A., D.D.

Of the Community of the Resurrection
Canon of Westminster

WIPF & STOCK · Eugene, Oregon

Wipf and Stock Publishers
199 W 8th Ave, Suite 3
Eugene, OR 97401

The Body of Christ
An Enquiry into the Institution and Doctrine of Holy Communion
By Gore, Charles
ISBN 13: 978-1-60608-263-8
Publication date 01/08/2009
Previously published by John Murray, 1901

PREFACE.

This enquiry into the institution and doctrine of the holy eucharist was first announced under the title of *The Breaking of the Bread;* but as it appeared that this title was already appropriated, *The Body of Christ* was chosen for a title, because it expresses two most important aspects of eucharistic truth. It expresses the nature of the gift presented to us in the sacrament (*corpus Christi*), and also the nature of the holy society of which it is the spiritual nourishment, and of which it is written, "Ye are the body of Christ."

It is important in the case of any enquiry to state what is its point of departure. I wish therefore to make it plain at starting that I assume the belief in Christ expressed in the Nicene Creed, and I assume also the substantial truth of the passages in the New Testament which bear upon the institution of the eucharist. (Thus, as a minor part of this assumption, it is taken for granted, though only incidentally, that however we deal with the apparent discrepancy between the synoptists and St. John, the eucharist must be allowed to have its roots, in some way, among the associations of the paschal meal.) There is of course at the present moment a most real and serious need to vindicate afresh the historical character of the Gospels: and the examination into their trustworthiness, which must be the basis of any such vindication, cannot be too stringent. But the task is not attempted in this volume. I must content myself with referring tó the thorough and impartial investigations of Dr. Sanday (see page 310).

I ought also to explain that I have not traversed again ground that I had gone over in a volume entitled *Dissertations*. I had there discussed (for instance) Tertullian's doctrine of the eucharist, and given quotations to illustrate the history of the doctrine of transubstantiation; and I have here simply referred to these discussions and quotations.[1]

---

[1] In both volumes Migne's *Patrologia Græca* and *Latina* are referred to as *P. G.* and *P. L.* with the number of the volume and column added.

PREFACE.

In the case of a book which does not claim to be a complete treatise, I hope that the full Table of Contents, prefixed to this volume, will be found as useful as an index.

I am very well aware that to some people, more or less theologically or ecclesiastically minded, this book will seem in part too indefinite, and to others of an opposite state of mind, if they should happen to read it, by far too definite. To the former I have said what I can in the course of the argument. To the latter I would take this opportunity of saying, that at a certain stage of religious progress it seems to be better not to attempt to think too accurately about the Holy Communion, but to use, with what faith and devotion is possible, a sacrament of which it was said at its institution, "*Do* this" (not "think this") "in remembrance of me." But when the mind has become habituated to the thought of the incarnation and of Christ's life communicated to us by the Spirit—a thought which holds so central a place in the New Testament—it ought to become possible, nay necessary, for us, to exercise our minds also upon the eucharist, and to gain as great clearness of intellectual apprehension upon this subject as upon any part of the divine method in the redemption of man.

I should like to add that this book is in part the result of an attempt to clear up my own thoughts on eucharistic subjects in view of the "Round Table Conference" to which I had been summoned by the late Bishop of London, whose loss the church has such profound reason to deplore; and my best prayer in sending it out is that it may serve in some measure the object of that Conference —the promotion of mutual understanding and unity among Christians.

CHARLES GORE.

WESTMINSTER ABBEY,
   Quinquagesima, 1901.

CONTENTS.

CHAPTER I.

PRELIMINARY.

	PAGE
§ 1. *The Christian sacrament*	1
the idea (Goethe)	2
the primitive celebration (Justin	3
§ 2. *The eucharist among other sacrifices*	12
root conception of sacrifice (W. R. Smith)	12
its development	15
§ 3. *The fundamental idea*	21
meaning of John vi.	21
(Dr. Westcott)	24
other passages of N. T.	26
(Dr. Moule)	27
intellectual problem	32
§ 4. *The sacramental principle*	36
spiritualism false and true	36
social meaning of sacraments	40

CHAPTER II.

THE GIFT AND PRESENCE IN HOLY COMMUNION.

§ 1. *The nature of the gift*	48
(Hooker, Waterland)	49
(Athanasius, Cyril Alex.)	54

CONTENTS.

§ 1—*continued.*

    (Hilary, Augustin, Leo) 56
    (Cyril J., Ignatius) 57
    (Thomassin's summary) 58
    exceptions—1. (Origen, etc.) . . . 59
              2. (Clement, Jerome, Ratramn, etc.) . . 60
              3. (Irenæus, Tertullian, etc.). 62
    the gift of the living, glorified, Christ . 66
    connection of eucharistic with baptismal gift (Fulgentius, etc.) 67

§ 2. *The relation of the spiritual gift to the bread and wine* 71
    the presence objective (Mozley) . . 72
    evidence—I. Treatment of elements . . 75
            II. The prayer of consecration . 76
                  general form (Clementine). 77
                  exceptions—
                      (1) words of institution not reckoned (Cyril J.) 80
                      (2) Holy Ghost not mentioned (Serapion, Irenæus) . . . 81
                      (3) vagueness as to what the elements become (Ethiopic, Gallican) . 82
                      (4) Roman canon . . 83
        (note on ποιεῖν, ἀποδείκνυναι, ἀποφαίνειν) . 79
            III. Language of fathers (Cyril J., Chrysostom) . . . 87

CONTENTS.

§ 2. Evidence III.—*continued*.

        localizing language . . 88
        meaning of "symbol" (Harnack, Greg. Nyss.) . . 89
        localization avoided (Optatus, Chrysostom) . 91
        (Newman) . . . 93
        conclusion on evidence . 93
    reason for objectivity 94
      as at Pentecost 95
  objections—
    (1) (*Didache*, etc.) 96
    (2) absence of the worship of Jesus in the consecrated elements . . 99
        evidence of liturgies . . . 100
        theologians (Chrys., Ambr., Aug., Cyril J., Theod.) . . . 103
        explanation of this absence—
        (1) Christ already present as priest 104
        (2) "Jesus-worship" not yet much developed . . 106
        (Hort, Talbot, Bigg, Westcott) 106
  conclusion 109

§ 3. *Transubstantiation considered* 111
  not the belief of fathers (Iren., Theod.) . 111
  monophysite tendency in East (Greg. Nyss., John of D.) 113
  not so in West (Augustine) . . . 115

CONTENTS.

	PAGE
§ 3—*continued.*	
but later it prevails (Berengar)	116
superstitious period	116
scholastic reaction	118
total result	120
§ 4. *The gift and presence spiritual*	124
meaning not merely "to our spirits" (J. Taylor)	124
nor "non-material"	125
but "that in which the purpose of the spirit unrestrictedly dominates".	126
the body of the risen Christ	127
application to the eucharistic presence	130
consequent necessity for observing the limits of the divine purpose	131
no hypostatical union of Christ with the elements	133
the purpose for which the sacrament was given	134
risk of going beyond it	136
the relation of the presence to the faith of the recipient	142
(Mozley, Aug., Orig., Cypr., Jer., Leo, Paschasius, Rupert)	143
objectivity in natural and spiritual world relative to persons	149
(note on degrees of presence)	153
answer to objections	153

CHAPTER III.

THE EUCHARIST A SACRIFICE.

	PAGE
§ 1. *The church's sacrifices*	157
the eucharist called a sacrifice (Didache, Justin, Iren.)	157
note on "bloodless sacrifices"	159
the Fathers on heathen and Jewish sacrifices	160
no further need for propitiation in Christian church	164
but room for other sacrifices (Ep. to Hebrews)	165
(Clem. Rom., Orig., Iren.)	169
relation of the church's sacrifice to the one sacrifice	173

§ 2. *No repetition of the sacrifice upon the cross* . . 174
    (Aug., Chrysost., P. Lombard, Aquinas) . 175
    eucharist in what sense called propitiatory
        (Orig., J. Taylor) 177
    uniqueness and sufficiency of the cross imperilled—
        in popular mediæval ideas . . . 178
        in post-Tridentine theology . . 179
        by doctrine of dead Christ in the sacrament (Rupert, Andrewes) . 181

§ 3. *The connection between the earthly and the heavenly offering* 185
    (1) earthly sacrifice accepted at heavenly altar (Roman canon, Iren., Paschas.) 186

CONTENTS.

§ 3—*continued.*
    (2) presence of heavenly Lamb amidst the worshipping church . . . 192
        intercessions postponed or repeated. 193
        (Cypr., Cyril J., Chrys., Cabasilas, Ambr., Bright, Wesleys) . . 194
    (3) sacrifice consummated in communion . 199
        (Aquinas) 201
        "natural" and "mystical" body . 204
        (Augustine, etc.) 206

§ 4. *Summary* 210
    note on intercession for non-Christians . 211
    the sacrifice an act of the whole body (P. Lombard) 213

CHAPTER IV.

OUR AUTHORITIES.

§ 1. *Mediæval authority* 215
    its defects 217
    use and abuse of ecclesiastical authority:
        our Lord's attitude 220
        appeal to scripture 222

§ 2. *Authority of the Reformation* 227
    appeal of Anglican church to catholic antiquity 227
    Anglican position as to—
        (1) eucharistic gift 229
        (2) objective presence (Keble, Arch. Temple) 230

CONTENTS.

§ 2—*continued.*

 (3) transubstantiation 235
 (4) presence spiritual (J. Taylor) . . 235
 (5) eucharistic sacrifice 236
§ 3. *Authority of the church at large.* . . 239
 the Bible and the church . . . 241
§ 4. *The test of scripture* 243
 as to (1) the eucharistic gift . . . 243
  "flesh" and "body" . . 244
 (2) the objective presence . . . 246
 (3) transubstantiation . . . 247
 (4) presence spiritual . . . 248
 (5) sacrifice (Ep. to Hebrews) . . 249
  Melchizedekian priesthood . 255
  St. Paul. Christ's institution . 262
 note on "shewing the Lord's death" . 263

CHAPTER V.

OUR PRESENT SERVICE OF HOLY COMMUNION.

Some subordinate doctrinal principles . . . 269
 (1) community of priest and people . . 270
  suppression of voice . . . 271
  veiling of altar 272
 (2) communion of people . . . 273
  Sunday and daily eucharist . . 275
  presence of non-communicants . 276
 (3) the eucharist and "the word" . . 278
 (4) communion in both kinds . . . 278
  the special gift of each kind (Raymund) 279

CHAPTER V.—*continued*.

	PAGE
Defects in our *anaphora* or canon	280
note on meaning of "oblations"	280
Need to restore corporate aspect of eucharist	286

APPENDED NOTES.

1. *Justin Martyr on the eucharistic "word of prayer"* 289
2. *Eating Christ's flesh explained to mean receiving His teaching* . 290
3. *The ritual of the Roman church* . 292
4. *Ignatius of Antioch on the eucharist* . 292
5. *The reverent care of the sacred elements in the early ages* . 293
6. *The language used by some of the fathers as to a change in the water of baptism and in the chrism, similar to the change in the eucharistic elements* 294
7. *Irenæus on the invocation* . 295
8. *Victorinus Afer on an objective presence of Christ in the eucharist* . 296
9. *Later Westerns on the spirituality of the eucharistic presence* . 296
10. *Reservation of the sacrament, and the treatment of it after communion* . 298
11. *Irenæus on the sacrifice in the eucharist* . 300
12. *Passages in the fathers where the immolation of Christ appears to be spoken of as repeated* . 302
13. *Errors current in the later middle ages about the sacrifices of masses* . 304
14. *Some later Roman teaching on the sacrifice of the altar* . 305

CONTENTS.   xvii

APPENDED NOTES—*continued*.

15. *The " glorious interchanges" of the eucharist* . 306
16. *Presence at the eucharist of non-communicants* . 307
17. *Effect of the Epistle to the Hebrews upon eucharistic doctrine in Ambrose and Chrysostom* 308
18. *The four N. T. accounts of the institution* . . 310
19. *The eucharist before the passion and after* . . 312
20. *On the sacrificial meaning of* ποιεῖν *and* ἀνάμνησις 312
21. *The social aspect of the sacraments* . . . 316

THE BODY OF CHRIST.

CHAPTER I.

PRELIMINARY.

§ 1. *The Christian sacrament.*

AT almost any point in the history of the Christian Church on which the eye rests, the worship, and in a great measure the life, of Christians is found centring upon a religious ceremony in which the chief point is the presenting before God, and blessing, and receiving in common, of bread and wine. And in spite of great differences in the ceremonial with which this sacrament has been celebrated, in spite of varying types of teaching with regard to it, which in later times of controversy have become acutely distinguished and opposed, the religious meaning attached to the rite on the whole has been remarkably similar everywhere and throughout history. As Goethe said, looking at the matter sympathetically, but, as we may say, from outside, "The sacraments are . . . the symbols to our souls of an extraordinary divine favour and grace. In the Lord's Supper earthly lips are to receive a divine reality embodied, and under the form of an earthly nourishment to partake of a heavenly. This idea is just the same in all Christian churches, whether the sacrament is taken with more or less submission to the mystery, with more or less accommodation to what is intelligible; it always remains a holy, weighty ceremony, which presents itself in the actual world in the place of [what one may call] the possible or the impossible—in the place of what man can neither attain nor do without."[1]

[1] Goethe, *Aus Meinem Leben* (Wahrheit and Dichtung), Th. ii. B. 7. (Bohn's trans. vol. i. pp. 245 f.) The context is a very interesting one. Goethe is emphasizing the need of habit and sequence in religion. From this point of view he is complaining of the paucity of Protestant sacraments. "Such a sacrament (as the Lord's Supper)

But from a point of view internal to the Christian faith, we may speak more exactly. The divine thing in this sacrament, the spiritual nourishment imparted, has been almost universally understood to be, in some real sense, the flesh and blood, or body and blood, of Christ; and by receiving it Christians have believed themselves to be bound into one, by being all together united to God in Christ. "The cup of blessing which we (Christians) bless," St. Paul had written, "is it not a communion in the blood of the Christ? The loaf which we break, is it not a communion in the body of the Christ? Seeing that there is one loaf, we the many are one body: for we all partake from the one loaf."[1]

To make this common idea of the Christian sacrament plainer at starting, we will read the very early account of it which Justin Martyr, in the middle of the second century, gave

should not stand alone (in the mature life); no Christian can partake of it with the true joy for which it is given, if the symbolical or sacramental sense is not fostered within him."

[1] 1 Cor. x. 16, 17. See R.V. margin.

to the Emperor Antoninus Pius, as a part of the "apology" by which he intended to disabuse the minds of the non-Christian world of their gross misconceptions of what Christianity meant.

After describing the ceremony of baptism, he continues thus [1]:—

"And after we have thus bathed the person who has become a believer and adherent, we lead him to the 'brethren,' as they are called, where they are assembled to offer up common prayers earnestly on behalf of themselves and the newly enlightened one and all others everywhere, that it may be vouchsafed to us who have learned the truth to be found also in our conduct good members of the society,[2] and keepers of the commandments, that we may be saved with the eternal salvation.

---

[1] *Apol.* 1, 65-6.

[2] The word is that of Phil. i. 27: "Let your *conversation* be as becometh the Gospel."—R. V. margin: "*Behave as citizens* worthily." "The word ... at this time," says Lightfoot, "seems always to refer to public duties devolving on a man as a member of a body." *Cf.* Phil. iii. 20; Ephes. ii. 19; and my *Ephesians*, p. 255.

Then when we have done our prayers we greet one another with a kiss. Then there is presented to the president of the brethren a loaf and a cup of water and wine ; and he, after taking them, offers up praise and glory to the Father of all things, through the name of the Son and of the Holy Spirit, and he gives thanks (eucharist) at length for these favours of God to us. And when he has ended the prayers and the thanksgiving (eucharist) the whole assistant people assent with an 'amen'—a Hebrew word meaning 'so be it.'" (This thanksgiving is described elsewhere as being made on behalf of the benefits of our redemption as well as our creation—for indeed "Jesus Christ our Lord gave us the eucharistic bread to offer for a memorial of the passion which He endured on behalf of the men whose souls were being cleansed from all wickedness."[1])
"And when the president has given thanks, and the whole people has assented, those who are called deacons (ministers) among us give a portion of the loaf and wine and

[1] *Dial. c. Tryph.* c. 41.

water, over which the thanksgiving has been made, to each of those who are present, and they take it away to those who are not.

"And this food is called among us eucharist,[1] and no one is allowed to partake of it unless he believes that what we teach is true, and has been washed in the laver for the remission of sins and for regeneration, and is living as Christ enjoined.[2] For we do not receive these things as common bread or common drink, but just as Jesus Christ our Saviour, by the word of God made flesh, had both flesh and blood for our salvation, so we have been taught that the food over which thanks have been given by the word of prayer which comes from Him—that food from which our blood and flesh are by assimilation nourished—is both the flesh

---

[1] The word eucharist, "thanksgiving," came very early to be applied to the whole service, and so to mean the "service or sacrifice of thanksgiving," and also (as here) the consecrated elements themselves, which formed, as it were, the material of the sacrifice of thanksgiving.

[2] We should note that the three qualifications for communion are: (1) elementary faith in the creed; (2) baptism; (3) good living.

and the blood of that Jesus who was made flesh."

The general meaning of this passage is plain. A divine word was the instrument in effecting the incarnation by which the Son of God took our human flesh and blood. And similarly in every eucharist a divine word — a word of prayer which Christ delivered—produces an analogous effect, *i.e.* an analogous union of the divine and the earthly. For the bread and wine—which correspond to the lower nature, the human flesh and blood, of the incarnation, and which indeed form by digestion the material of our common flesh and blood—become, when blessed and consecrated, something higher and diviner, the spiritual food of the flesh and blood of Christ.[1]

Then Justin continues: "For the apostles delivered, in the memoirs compiled by them, which are called Gospels, that this command was given to them—that Jesus took bread

---

[1] As to what exactly Justin Martyr means by the "prayer-word which is from Christ," by which the eucharist is blessed, see app. note 1, p. 289.

and gave thanks and said, 'Do[1] this in remembrance of me: this is my body'; and took the cup likewise and gave thanks and said, 'This is my blood'; and imparted it to them only. And in the mysteries of Mithra the evil spirits have instituted by imitation a similar rite; for you either know or can learn how in their ceremonies of initiation bread and a cup of water are produced with certain invocations."

Then after the first communion with the newly baptized Justin goes on to describe the ordinary Sunday service of the church, beginning with reading of scriptures, and a sermon preached by their "president," and common prayer. "And, as we said before, when the prayers are over, bread is produced and wine and water, and the president offers up prayers and thanksgivings, according to his power [the forms of prayer, we observe, were not yet fixed]; and the people assent with the 'amen,' and the distribution and

---

[1] Justin Martyr (alone, apparently, among early Christian writers) understands this word as meaning *offer*. See below, p. 314.

participation by each of the blessed food takes place, and it is sent away to those who are not present by the hands of the deacons. . . . And if all this seems to you to be agreeable to truth and reason, hold it in honour. But if it seems to you trifling, then as trifles despise it, but do not, as if we were enemies, decree death against us when we are doing no harm."

A modern reader will probably feel that this is an exceedingly interesting, ingenuous and matter-of-fact account of Christian worship—an account which, on the whole, could hardly fail to be conciliatory to the more enlightened or unprejudiced heathen. No doubt Justin repeats the phrases about eating and drinking the body (or flesh) and blood of Christ, which had been a great occasion of blasphemy; but they would have been felt to require some mystical interpretation as remote as possible from cannibalism. And yet this idea of eating Christ's flesh and drinking His blood in the eucharist—which, we observe, Justin here puts forward without any hesitation before the heathen as the accepted Christian idea—is, for the imaginative or speculative intellect, a very difficult one. As soon as the church began to speculate about it she found its difficulty. All the more remarkable, therefore, is the devotional unanimity on the subject of this sacrament which characterized the church for some eleven centuries, and which, even since acute controversy began, has characterized, and still characterizes, the devotional attitude or feelings of pious Christians, very much more than the antagonism of combatants would lead us to believe. At this moment in history, so far as Christians are content with believing, and feeling, and using the Holy Communion devoutly as an appointed means of grace, there is probably a surprising unanimity amongst them.

But on this, as on every other important subject, it is necessary, even at the risk of controversy, to let devout feeling pass into as much clearness of intellectual apprehension and expression as the case admits of; or, where we cannot gain any such clearness, to perceive at least that this intellectual limitation is no more than must be recognized in other directions, and for similar reasons. We must at least seek to understand as well as to believe. And we will make a beginning of our attempt to understand the Christian mystery of the breaking of the bread with the considerations suggested by Justin's hint of its resemblance to one of the rites of Mithra—the consideration, that is to say, of its affinities with the customs of religion in general outside the area of the special revelation which is the basis of the Christian church. We will approach the eucharist first from outside.

§ 2. *The eucharist among other sacrifices.*

The sacrificial feast of Christians,—for so they conceived it from the earliest times,—has an obvious affinity with almost universal practices in other religions. Most religions have centred in sacrificial rites, which have commonly culminated in sacrificial banquets. From a variety of causes we to-day naturally associate with sacrifice the idea of *giving* something to some being believed to be divine, whether in order to propitiate his anger, or to maintain intercourse with him, or to recognize his claim upon his worshippers. But recent investigation has tended to show that at least one deep root of sacrificial customs, if not *the* root, is the idea of communion or common sharing in a life believed to be divine. "We may now take it as made out," writes Dr. Robertson Smith,[1] "that throughout the Semitic

[1] *Religion of the Semites* (Black, 1889), pp. 327, 418; *cp.*

SACRIFICES IN GENERAL.

field [the group of races to which the Jews belonged] the fundamental idea of sacrifice is not that of a sacred tribute, but of communion between the god and his worshippers by joint participation in the living flesh and blood of a sacred victim." "The one point that comes out clear and strong is that the fundamental idea of ancient sacrifice is sacramental communion, and that all atoning rites are ultimately to be regarded as owing their efficacy to a communication of divine life to the worshipper, and to the establishment or confirmation of a living bond between them and their God."

We must endeavour to grasp this thought. The tribe or family, or later some group of voluntarily initiated worshippers, believes some plant or animal or thing to be divine, or to be temporarily the habitation of the divine presence; and in consuming this, the divine life is believed to pass into them

Encycl. Brit. (9th ed.) *s.v.* SACRIFICE, vol. xxi. p. 138, for some excellent remarks on the religious value of savage ideas.

all in common, and to strengthen with a religious bond their social unity. As more refined ideas of the divine being make such identification of a god with anything that can be eaten or drunk more difficult, the unquenchable desire for divine communion through eating takes the form of supposing that the god and his worshippers feast together; as, for example, when part of a sacrifice is burnt, and so rises up in a smoke believed to be acceptable to the god, and thus becomes his "bread,"[1] or again is eaten by the priests as representing the god, while the residue is consumed by the worshippers, who thus feast, if not upon, yet with, their god. It is well known that in the case of the peace offerings of the Jews the greater part of the meat of the sacrifice was eaten by the worshippers;[2] and, though it is never expressly stated, the probability is that the idea was that of communion with Jehovah.

[1] Levit. xxi. 6, 8, 17, 21.

[2] It is plain (Levit. vii. 15—21) that the eating was part of the sacrifice. See ver. 18, and *cp*. Deut. xvi. 2, 3: "Thou shalt *sacrifice* the passover unto the Lord. . . . Thou shalt *eat* no leavened bread with it."

Thus the "altar" was also called the "table" of the Lord.[1]

On the whole, it is no doubt the case that the development of the sacrificial system among the Jews tended to bring to the front the idea of giving to God in homage and recognition, and propitiating Him by victims, at the expense of the idea of communion with Him. And the reason is most interesting. In the old natural religions there had been little sense of the moral holiness of the god worshipped. Consequently "the relations of man to the gods were not troubled by any habitual and oppressive sense of human guilt." It was hardly conceivable that the god could be permanently alienated from his worshippers, for they belonged to one another naturally. The conditions for communion with him were physical and ceremonial. But the Jews were to be taught a new lesson—the awful moral holiness of Jehovah, their God, and the necessity of being morally like Him in order to approach Him. And they had to be taught this lesson

[1] Ezek. xli. 22, xliv. 16; Mal. i. 7—12.

by the discipline of fear. The traditional easy-going familiarity with the tribal god was over. They were to fear Jehovah. This fear was inculcated in part by the moral law and teaching of Moses and his successors, the prophets; in part by divine events and startling judgments; but also in part by the way in which the ceremonial law, as it was gradually elaborated, fenced the chosen people off from God, and made them realize the awfulness of His presence.

But the closeness of communion with God had been taken away from God's own people only to be given back on a truer and surer basis. When once they had learned to fear God's righteousness, that very righteousness was to manifest itself to them as a love communicating itself and welcoming them into closest and most indissoluble fellowship. Prophecy had anticipated this, and the New Testament is full of it. In fact, the idea of communion with God through Christ, the partaking of His life, the living in His life, is a central idea of the New Testament. There

SACRIFICES IN GENERAL.

are certainly some difficulties belonging to a famous passage in the Epistle to the Hebrews which speaks of the "altar" which Christians have, "whereof they have no right to eat which serve the tabernacle."[1] But there can be no doubt that it is intended to point the contrast between the old covenant and the new from this particular point of view, that under the old covenant with the Jews not even the priests could eat of their great sin offering of the Day of Atonement, but that under the new covenant, of which Jesus is the mediator, that sacrifice by which atonement was made for us is also that in which we are admitted to share. Christ our propitiation is also our new life, and He can be the former in a true sense only because He is the latter. Thus we Christians do truly (in whatever sense) eat the flesh of Christ offered for us and drink His outpoured blood, and are thus, through fellowship in the manhood of Christ, made partakers of the divine nature which is also His.

[1] Heb. xiii. 10.

From this point of view the Christian eucharist, or "bloodless sacrifice" as it was called—the presenting before God and consecrating the loaf and the wine (very commonly recognized elements of sacrifice), and then the common partaking of this consecrated food by the whole church, with the belief that in this sacrament or sacred rite a divine life was, in some mystical sense, partaken of and divine fellowship enjoyed—this Christian eucharist, I say, would, so far, have appeared an easily intelligible rite to the well-disposed enquirers of the Roman Empire. As to its origin, indeed, it was wholly Jewish, not heathen. Any other suggestion is quite unhistorical. It was developed out of the rites and associations of the paschal sacrifice and meal. But the passover of the Jews, with their other sacrificial rites, was akin to religious customs which are universal. Thus both in the national religions and in the private mysteries of the Empire sacrifices more or less barbaric or refined, which consisted in or culminated in sacramental communion, were thoroughly familiar.[1] Their familiarity must indeed be assumed to render intelligible Augustine's repeated definition of sacrifice as "any act that is done in order by a holy fellowship to inhere in God."[2] Thus, as we look back, we recognize in the eucharist, in its outward form no less than in its inward idea, the divine consecration of an instinct belonging to what, in the most historical sense, we can call natural religion. Here is something easily appreciable by all men—the sacrificial meal upon the food which symbolizes for civilized man strength and refreshment—the "bread that strengthens," and "the wine that maketh glad the heart of man." And

---

[1] *Cf.* F. B. Jevons' *Introduction to the Study of Religion* (Methuen), cc. xii. and xxiii., which are largely based on Robertson Smith, *op. cit.* Among older writers see John Johnson's *Unbloody Sacrifice* (in the "Libr. of Anglo-Cath. Theol.") ii. pp. 43 ff. In the passage from Justin Martyr cited above, he points to the resemblance between the eucharist and the very widely-spread rites of Mithra; but he attributes to Satanic imitation what we should attribute to a universal human instinct, inspired and used by God both under the types of the old covenant and under the sacraments of the new.

[2] *De Civ.* x. 5, 6.

the ideas underlying the sacramental meal have shown the power which belongs to the deepest human ideas, to grow with man's growth, and not to become antiquated.

§ 3. *The fundamental idea.*

It is a broadly human idea, then, this which Goethe describes as "partaking of heavenly under the form of earthly nourishment"; and yet, in its Christian form, it is not easy to realize with any intelligence—not easy especially for the somewhat sluggish imagination of us Englishmen. What does it mean—this "eating the flesh of Christ and drinking His blood"? Apart from any question as to how we do this in the eucharist, what is the idea which the words are intended to convey to our minds; or again, St. Paul's similar phrase, "the communion in the body and blood of Christ"?[1]

On the one hand, we shall not be satisfied with any explanation of eating Christ's flesh and blood, or body and blood, which makes it a metaphor for believing in Him or receiving

[1] The reasons for not making any broad distinction between "flesh" and "body" are stated below, pp. 244 ff.

His words.[1] A metaphor or parable must really illustrate what it is intended to explain. Our Lord's metaphors and parables do this pre-eminently and justly. He never, as many of His interpreters have since done, over-presses the figure. But if "eating Christ's flesh and drinking His blood" were merely a figure for believing in Him, it would be, as insisted upon in the discourse in St. John vi., an overpressed and misleading figure. Moreover, as we examine the argument of that discourse, we see that the heavenly food of the flesh and blood of Christ is not an equivalent for faith, but is the divine response to it or satisfaction of it. Faith in the Christ is the "work" that God demands of men: the true manna, the bread of life, the flesh and blood of Christ, is the divine gift given to faith, corresponding to the wages given for work. Faith admits to the gift, but is not the same thing with it. Rather, the gift satisfies the spiritual appetite of faith, as the manna satisfied the physical appetite.[2]

---

[1] On this misapprehension, see app. note 2, p. 290.
[2] See John vi. 27—29, 47—51, 58.

The flesh and blood of Christ, then, mean a gift, corresponding with the manna—a heavenly food given by God to man, which faith receives but does not create, and which it cannot do without.

On the other hand, our Lord, as reported by St. John, guarded against the disciples misunderstanding in any gross sense the meaning of His flesh and blood. He directed their attention away from the flesh and blood of His mortal and corruptible body upward to His future glory. "What and if ye shall see the Son of Man ascending where he was before?"[1] He told them that in the ordinary sense human flesh could do them no good—"the flesh profiteth nothing": that only spirit could impart true life to man, and that the flesh and blood He had been speaking of —the flesh and blood of the Son, ascended and glorified—could impart life to them only because they truly were spirit and life. Thus He lifted their minds to a high and spiritual region, where they could be in no danger of low and carnal misconceptions. He "diverts

[1] John vi. 60—64.

them," as Athanasius says, "from a bodily conception."[1] But none the less, He plainly means them to understand that, in some sense, *His manhood is to be imparted to those that believe in Him, and fed upon as a principle of new and eternal life.* There is to be an "influence" in the original sense of the word—an inflowing of His manhood into ours. Nothing less than this can be meant by feeding on His flesh.[2] Shall we say, then,

[1] *Ad Serap.* iv. 19. See my *Dissertations*, p. 305.

[2] *Cf.* Westcott, *Rev. of the Father*, p. 40: "Now it is easy to say that 'eating of the flesh of Christ,' is a figurative way of describing faith in Christ. But such a method of dealing with the words of Holy Scripture is really to empty them of their divine force. This spiritual eating, this feeding upon Christ, is the best result of faith, the highest energy for faith, but it is not faith itself. To eat is to take that into ourselves which we can assimilate as the support of life. The phrase 'to eat the flesh of Christ' expresses therefore, as perhaps no other language could express, the great truth that Christians are made partakers of the human nature of their Lord which is united in one person to the divine nature, that He imparts to us now, and that we can receive into our own manhood, something of His manhood, which may be the seed, so to speak, of the glorified bodies in which we shall hereafter behold Him. Faith, if I may so express it, in its more general sense, leaves us outside Christ trusting in Him; but the crowning act of faith incorporates us in Christ."

that by His flesh we understand the spiritual principle or essence of His manhood, as distinguished from its material constituents? and by His blood, according to the deeply-rooted Old Testament idea, the "life thereof"[1] —the human life of Jesus of Nazareth in His glory? Whether these phrases are thought to be satisfactory or no, in some sense it is the manhood which must be meant by the flesh and blood.

At the same time, it is equally evident that it is only because of the vital unity in which the manhood stands with the divine nature that it can be " spirit " and " life." It is the humanity of nothing less than the divine person which is to be, in some sense, communicated to us, and not (what would be the worst materialism) a separated flesh and blood. What the Father is spoken of as giving us is the whole Christ—the whole of

[1] Levit. xvii. 11, 14 (R. V.) : " The life (or 'soul') of the flesh is in the blood ; and I have given it to you upon the altar to make atonement for your souls; for it is the blood that maketh atonement by reason of the life. . . . As to the life of all flesh, the blood thereof is all one with the life thereof. . . . The life of all flesh is the blood thereof."

His indivisible and living self. "As the living Father sent me, and I live because of the Father: so he that eateth me, he also shall live because of me. This is the bread which came down out of heaven."[1]

The glorified Son of Man, then, Christ Jesus—the Word and Son of the Father made flesh and glorified — is to impart His own life to believers, and by this alone can they hope to share in the true eternal life. This is the central idea of St. John vi. Nothing less than this can justify the startling emphasis laid in the discourse upon eating Christ's flesh and drinking His blood. And the idea is in agreement with the teaching of the last discourses of our Lord as St. John also reports them. There too it appears that the future coming of the Spirit as the substitute for Christ—the new advocate—is to involve a coming of Christ also Himself in a new way. The Father, our Lord says, will send "another advocate," but also—"I come unto you;" "Because I live, ye shall live also;" "I am the vine, ye are the

[1] John vi. 57.

branches;" "Abide in me, and I in you."[1] Plainly, all this language is exaggerated and excessive, unless this is to be a characteristic function of the Spirit in the church, to communicate and so perpetuate the life of the glorified Christ as the new life of the new society of believers.

As Dr. Moule says, "I see in them [such words as those just cited] a remembrance that what the Spirit does in His free and all-powerful work in the soul which He guides into new life, is, above all things, to bring it into contact with the Son. He roots it, He grafts it, He embodies it into the Son. He deals so with it that there is a continuity wholly spiritual indeed, but none the less most real, unfigurative and efficacious, between the Head and the limb, between the branch and the Root. He effects an influx into the regenerate man of the blessed virtues of the nature of the second Adam, an infusion of the exalted life of Jesus Christ, through an open duct, living and divine, into the man who is born

[1] John xiv. 16—19, xv. 1, 4—6.

again into Him, the incarnate and glorified Son of God." [1]

And that Christ did really speak language of the kind referred to by St. John, is postulated, I cannot but think, by the narrative of the institution of the eucharist in the Synoptic Gospels, and by the language which St. Paul finds ready to his hand. By the language of the Synoptic Gospels, I say, at the institution of the eucharist, for the eucharist I suppose to be the appointed means for realizing a relationship to Christ already described in St. John vi. Such unexampled language as "Take eat: this is my body . . . Drink this: this is my blood," can hardly have stood isolated and unexplained; and with the most inevitable directness of force, it implies that it is Christ's manhood of which we are to partake. And this is the idea also upon which St. Paul works.[2] It appears in his writings as the revealed ground of his teaching about the

[1] Moule, *Veni Creator* (Hodder and Stoughton), pp. 39 f.
[2] See (in order) 1 Cor. xi. 23—26, x. 16—18, xii. 12, 27, Col. i. 18, ii. 19, Ephes. i. 23.

relation of Christ to the church which is His body. We need not stop to enquire whether in using the term "the body of Christ" for the Christian society, St. Paul had chiefly in mind the organic unity of the visible society as a body of many members, or the fact that what constituted its unity was the communicated life of Christ the head; whether, that is to say, the metaphor, as St. Paul used it, was mainly social, as in other literature, or mainly Christological. Apparently it was at different periods mainly the one or mainly the other. But it is impossible to consider St. Paul's language where he explains to us what he received "from the Lord" about the institution of the perpetual memorial of Christ, and emphasizes the awful sacredness of the bread and cup which are there presented to us;[1] or where he speaks of the vital unity of the church, as constituted and expressed by the communion in Christ's body and blood;[2] or where he speaks of being baptized

[1] 1 Cor. xi. 23 to end.
[2] 1 Cor. x. 16—17.

into the church as baptism "into Christ Jesus";[1] or of Christ in His glorified manhood as "life-giving spirit";[2] or of the whole new life of the Church as "in Christ,"[3] —it is impossible, I say, to consider all this language without feeling that what St. Paul believed in was not a bare or mere gift of a divine Spirit to the church, but a gift of the divine Spirit with this for His special function—to communicate the nature of the glorified Christ, and to perpetuate in the world His divine and human life. Christ is our example and our outward pattern: He is again our propitiation with the Father: but He is also our new life. And what makes His example practicable for us in spite of the gulfs of difference which separate His sinlessness from our sinfulness and His glory from our shame, is the fact that He is not only outside us as an example in the history of the remote past, but alive and at work in us at the present moment,

---

[1] Rom. vi. 3.
[2] 1 Cor. xv. 45.
[3] 2 Cor. v. 17.

moulding us inwardly into His likeness. Again, what makes it morally possible that Christ should have acted and offered Himself vicariously for us once for all, is the fact that He who thus offered Himself as man was to become the head of a new race, and those for whom He offered Himself were to belong to His manhood and share its power and its motive. This—the propagation of Christ's manhood by the transmission of His Spirit, or Christ *in us* the hope of glory—is truly the culminating point of our religion, which alone explains the rest. It was felt to be so at least through all the first twelve centuries of our era.

But it will be said, Why labour this point?—is it not universally agreed? Among theologians, perhaps, it is a common-place, and among Christians of a certain kind. But it remains very difficult language to a great many Englishmen. And it is the lack of this fundamental conception of the life of the Son of Man imparted to His people by the Spirit, which makes it so difficult to secure a really vital belief in this particular sacrament of Christ's body and blood. We must labour to secure for it a fundamental lodgment. We must try and get the intelligence on to its side.

By eating Christ's flesh is meant, as we have seen, receiving into ourselves and appropriating by faith what we can only describe as the spiritual principle of His manhood; and by "drinking His blood," receiving and absorbing His human but God-united life. No doubt it may be said that language like this appeals rather to the spiritual *imagination* and *feeling* of believers than to their speculative intellect. No doubt also in its warmth and fulness it appeals to some more naturally than to others—to St. Paul rather than to St. James, to Ignatius of Antioch rather than to Clement of Rome; but no one can be at home in the New Testament language as a whole without being able to dwell on it and give a meaning to it; and it may be doubted whether, when we come to examine it, the idea involves any more intellectual difficulty than is involved in the mystery of human

THE FUNDAMENTAL IDEA.

life at its inception and at every stage of its propagation.

We know that our human life is not an isolated product in each individual. We men belong to a family, to a race, to humanity: that is to say, we derive our life with all its wonderful faculties and faults—not only physical but intellectual, moral and spiritual —from our parents and ancestors, back to the beginnings of our race. We share a common and a transmitted life.[1] The process of its transmission—the manner in which we individuals carry in ourselves not only the physical stock but the accumulated moral and spiritual heritage of the manhood to which we belong—this permeation of the individual by the race, is very mysterious. It baffles our attempts at analysis at every turn. It does not enable us fully to interpret and explain the phenomena of individuality which stand out against the fact of unity,

---

[1] I touch here the edge of the old controversy between traducianism and creationism. But I think, however much emphasis we may lay on the individuality of each soul, something like what is stated above must be admitted.

still less to forecast or anticipate them. But it is a fact. It is the justifying principle of St. Paul's teaching about the "first Adam"— this fact of our natural organic unity. And we must ask whether there is really anything more mysterious or intellectually difficult in the conception of the second Adam, of the glorified Christ, healing the spiritual and moral unsoundness of the human race by infusing into it, through whatever means, the recreative influences of His own manhood. Nor will a reasonable man be surprised that he cannot subject these influences of the new manhood to analysis, for he cannot subject life to analysis at any stage, so as to find out its secret.

Thus we return and take our stand upon what the language of the New Testament involves—that Christ declared His intention to communicate to His church His own human life; that the apostles who first fully expounded His intentions believed and taught this, and transmitted the belief to the best and deepest of Christians in all generations; and that it is this which alone makes intelligible the whole of the Christian language about the eucharist, which goes back for its certificate to the institution of Christ. This fundamental principle must be our first presupposition in approaching the doctrine of the eucharist.

§ 4. *The sacramental principle.*

Our second presupposition must be some adequate perception of the meaning and value of sacraments; a condition of mind such as renders it intelligible that a spiritual gift should be communicated by God to man through the medium of a material ceremony.

There is, it must be admitted, a tendency in Protestantism, partly to be explained by reaction, towards a conception of spirituality which is certainly not completely Christian— a conception which puts the spiritual straight off in opposition to the material, so that the idea of a spiritual gift attached by divine ordinance to material conditions is rejected as unworthy of God.[1] It is questionable whether those who hold such language can ever have really reflected on the conditions under which indisputably the most important

[1] *Cf.* Mr. W. Hay M. H. Aitken, *The Mechanical versus the Spiritual* (Shaw, 1899).

and fundamental spiritual gift given on this earth, the gift which is the necessary foundation of all others—the gift of the human soul, capable of all spiritual activities, and destined for an immortal fellowship with God —is actually given. The production on this earth of a human soul or personality, with all its tremendous and eternal possibilities for good and evil, is by God's creative will indisputably attached to material conditions; and such conditions as are in experience found to be the most liable to be misused, and to become not material only but carnal. This at least gives us something to think about. It shows us something of the mind of God. This dependence of the immortal spirit — the only seat of human spirituality—upon material conditions, at its origin and throughout its existence upon the earth, is the most convincing refutation of a great deal of language used in repudiation of the sacramental principle.

So inextricably, in fact, is the human spirit implicated in the flesh, that it is only through the perceptions of the senses that it is able originally to act at all; and in the relations of men to one another their life is carried on, to an extent which reflection leads us to realize more and more, upon a basis of what one may call natural sacraments. Thus handshaking is the sacrament of friendship, and kissing the sacrament of love. And each in expressing also intensifies the emotion which it expresses. The spirit in us feeds upon the material of its own symbols. The flag again is the sacrament of the soldiers' honour, and can stimulate it to the point of uttermost self-sacrifice. And it would be easy to go on multiplying such examples. Thus there can be no doubt that, on all human analogy, a religion which, like the Christian religion, exists to realize communion with God under conditions of ordinary human life, and which refuses to confine its message to some select class of philosophers who may claim (though it is an idle boast) to live a life aloof from the body—such a religion for common men must have developed, apart from any question of authority, sacramental ceremonies.

THE SACRAMENTAL PRINCIPLE. 39

They are, as all history shows, the natural means for religion to use.

Would then the divine principles of the Christian religion hinder such use of sacraments? On the contrary, the religion of the incarnation—the religion of a Christ come in the flesh—associates the lower and material nature with the whole process of redemption, and teaches us that not without a material and visible embodiment is the spiritual life to be realized either now or in eternity. The spiritual, in the New Testament, means not what is separated from the material or the bodily, but that in which the spirit rules, or that which expresses a spiritual meaning.[1] Thus from the days when the first Christian Fathers were fighting their great battle against the false spirituality of Gnosticism, it has been the sound argument of Christian theologians[2] that the idea of sacraments—the idea of spiritual gifts given through material means — is of a

[1] See further, p. 126.
[2] See Ignatius *ad Smyrn.* 6; Irenæus *c. hær.* i. 21, 4, v. 17—18, v. 2—3; Tertullian *de res. carn.* 8; Gregory of

piece with the whole method of God in the creation and redemption of man; of a piece, to put the matter otherwise, with the twofold nature of man, in which the body is associated most intimately with every spiritual faculty, and in which every spiritual emotion and capacity is made to depend upon external and physical facts.

But the argument is enormously strengthened when the *social* character of sacraments is had in view. I suppose that if we ask ourselves the tremendous question why God, almighty and all-loving, should have attached the production of a spiritual personality, so awfully endowed, to conditions so precarious and capable of degradation as sexual union, the most satisfactory answer is, that this is but one example of a universal law: that God has willed (in spite of all the risks involved) to bind individual beings together in social relationship. God may indeed ultimately

---

Nyssa *cat. mag.* 33—35; Chrysostom *in Matt. hom.* lxxxii. 4. P. G. lvii. 743. These passages, read in their continuity, show a remarkable unity of teaching, and it would be easy to add to them.

take the soul into His own absolutely equitable hands, to reconstitute it solely in view of its individual possibilities and responsibilities; but for this world, at least, its whole condition, spiritual as well as material, is, to a degree which it is not easy to exaggerate, dependent upon the society which is responsible for it, whether it be family, tribe or nation. That the individual is to be the product of the society, not indeed wholly, but mainly and in most cases, is, I say, the lesson which universal nature bears upon its face.

And this law passes unchanged into the kingdom of redemption. There, also, the individual Christian is to be what he is, and to become what he can become, by relations to the divine society, the church. And it is in the method by which he is first brought into "the household," and then fed there, that this is apparent. That is to say, the sacraments, which are means of personal grace, are also social ceremonies: ceremonies only possible among members of a society.[1] The attachment of the particular spiritual gifts,

[1] See more at length app. note 21, pp. 316 ff.

by divine institution, to sacraments—that is, to social ceremonies—is the divine provision against spiritual individualism. Thus our new birth into Christ is attached to a washing of water. This is the "bath of regeneration," the being "baptized into Christ." But it is also our introduction into the society; "by one Spirit were we all baptized into one body." Again, our confirmation, or "unction" by the Holy Ghost, which is the completion of our baptism, is attached to the laying-on of the hands of the chief pastor of the society; and while it is the enriching of our personal life, it is also our investiture with a kingship and priesthood, which imply the full privileges and obligations of membership in the society. Once more, the fullest personal fellowship with Christ, the eating His flesh and drinking His blood, is attached to the pre-eminently social sacrament—that is to say, to "the breaking of the bread," the fraternal sharing of bread and wine.

At first the social aspect of the eucharist was unmistakable. As when it was instituted at the last supper, so when it was celebrated in the first days at Corinth, it was the crowning event of a special social meal—the "Lord's supper."[1] It thus extended its consecrating influence over all meals which were "sanctified by the word of God and prayer."[2] But human weakness very soon made such a mode of celebrating it undesirable. The Corinthians by their selfishness and greediness treated the supper as "their own" and not "the Lord's." Thus very early the eucharist had to be detached from the love-feast, and pursued its own independent development. In our day we could not wish it otherwise. Such a convivial background to the highest

[1] See 1 Cor. xi. 20. The "Lord's supper" appears to have been a name current for the meal, of which the eucharist formed a part. As a name for the eucharist alone it does not occur till much later—first in St. Basil. It must be remarked, that St. Paul's tremendous language (1 Cor. xi. 27—30) makes it impossible to suggest that—so far as the apostolic teaching went—the spiritual meaning of the eucharist was in any way imperilled by its social setting. But in the *Didache* we probably have an example of a half-Christianized church where this was the case.

[2] 1 Tim. iv. 4, 5. There are many indications in early days how the consecration spread itself from the "Christian sacrifice" over all Christian meals.

spiritual acts could only be maintained in societies which are kept at a very high level by the moral cost involved in joining them. But the social symbolism of the "breaking of the bread" was still apparent in Justin Martyr's days and later on,[1] especially in the dignified ritual of the Roman church. For there the primitive custom survived into the middle ages of taking the elements for consecration out of the offerings of the people; and also the special solemnity of the "fraction" of the consecrated bread, and the sending of portions from the bishop's mass to the other city churches, gave vivid expression to the unity of the body.[2] And even where the social symbolism of the

[1] The idea is ritually expressed by the breaking of the one loaf and the drinking of the one cup. Also, as Cyprian explains it to us, by the addition of water (representing us men) to the wine (of Christ's humanity). Might we not nowadays have a compromise in the Church of England by which one side should abandon the wholly unsymbolical practice of *separate* wafers in favour of the one bread, in some form leavened or unleavened; and the other side should accept the mixture of the chalice—indisputably a quite primitive custom?

[2] See app. note 3, p. 292.

THE SACRAMENTAL PRINCIPLE.

ritual was less pronounced, still in all parts of the world the teaching of the church gave to the idea more or less of emphasis.

We ought to remember that a great deal is lost—more than can be easily calculated—if at any period this great idea of fraternity is allowed to fade out of the eucharistic language or ritual of the church. A system hardly deserves the name of Christian at all, which does not impress upon its worshippers that communion with God is no otherwise to be realized than in human brotherhood.

The more we dwell on the social meaning of sacraments, the more profoundly satisfying an answer does it supply to the difficulties raised by such a false spiritualism as resents the attachment of spiritual gifts to outward conditions. On the other hand, there is here no disparagement of the claim which Christianity makes upon the individual will and heart and intellect. Our social opportunities, whether they be political or religious, are only realized by the response of the individual will—by the reaction of the man upon his surroundings. For example, the greater the birthright which belongs to an Englishman because of the circumstances of his birth, the greater the responsibility in which he is involved, and the more manifest the failure if he is apathetic or worse. Similarly also the greater the spiritual opportunities of our baptism, the deeper the requirement upon the faith of the individual to claim and use them; if need be, to be converted or "turn," and use them.[1] And the higher the gift which mere outward participation in the sacrament of the holy communion puts at our disposal, the more certain it is that only according to our faith will it be done to us. For faith only can appropriate and make our own a spiritual gift. But there will be further opportunities for reflecting upon this side of the truth when we come to speak of the presence in the eucharist as a *spiritual* presence.

And again, this doctrine of sacraments seeks to impose no restrictions on God,

---

[1] The true teaching is expressed by Gregory of Nyssa in few words in *cat. mag.* c. 36. Our salvation in its beginning is by "faith and water."

whether for this life or beyond it. God is not tied by His own ordinances, but can give where and as it pleases Him. We do but declare that the sacramental method is the stated and normal law of His kingdom, and therefore the law to which we at least are bound, alike in prudence and in love, to conform our practice and our expectations.

We are now in a position to give closer attention to the exact nature of the gift or presence in the eucharist, on the basis of these two presuppositions: (1) that a central and essential feature of the Christian religion is the communication to believers by the Spirit of the life of the Christ, divine and human, or, as we may call it, the spiritual principle and virtue of His manhood; (2) that the communication of this spiritual life to us by means of a material and social ceremony is quite analogous to the whole of what we know about the relation of the human spirit to bodily conditions, about the relation of the individual to the society, and about the principles of the pre-eminently human and social religion of the Son of Man.

CHAPTER II.

THE GIFT AND PRESENCE IN HOLY COMMUNION.

§ 1. *The nature of the gift.*

Now we are in a position to examine somewhat more definitely the nature of the gift given in Holy Communion. And at once we realize that on this—the most important matter—there has been comparatively little controversy. It is as to the relation of this divine gift or presence to the outward elements of bread and wine that controversy has raged in one form or another since the eleventh century with not much intermission. In England since the Reformation the question has chiefly been—Is the spiritual presence *in* the bread and wine independently of reception? or is it simply that a spiritual gift, as in baptism, accompanies a symbolical act—in this case an act of

THE NATURE OF THE GIFT.

feeding? This question will come forward for consideration immediately. At present we are only interested in the prior question —what is the spiritual gift given in Holy Communion; and about this there has been, as was said just now, comparatively little controversy. The gift of the eucharist is precisely that gift of the flesh, or body, and blood of Christ,—the spiritual principle and life of Christ's manhood, inseparable from His whole living self—the meaning of which, apart from all question of how or when we receive it, we were just now considering.

To prove a high degree of agreement on this point, I will proceed to cite a few typical witnesses. And as Richard Hooker stands specially for the attempt to decline or shelve what he describes as *the only controverted question*—that of a presence in the elements independently of reception—let Hooker first bear his witness as to the nature of the gift given, according to what he calls "the general agreement."[1]

[1] *Eccl. Pol.* V. lxvii. [2].

Christ in the sacrament, he declares, "imparteth Himself, even His whole entire person, as a mystical head, unto every soul that receiveth Him. . . . What merit, force or virtue soever there is in His sacrificed body and blood we freely, fully and wholly have it by this sacrament;" and "because the sacrament being but a corruptible and earthly creature must needs be thought an unlikely instrument to work so admirable effects on man, we are therefore to rest ourselves altogether upon the strength of His glorious power who is able and will bring to pass that this bread and cup which He giveth us shall be truly the thing He promiseth." Again he says, " The Sacramentaries" [that is, the schools of Zwingli and Calvin] "grant that these holy mysteries . . . impart to us in true and real though mystical manner the very person of our Lord Himself, whole, perfect and entire."[1]

Waterland, again, is a cautious and cold theologian of the eighteenth century,

[1] *L.c.* [7] and [8].

THE NATURE OF THE GIFT.

who is specially identified with the positive repudiation of any presence of Christ in the elements: but as to the spiritual effect of the act of communion his language is precise. It is a union with Christ's flesh and blood, *i.e.*, His manhood, and so it is "a mystical union with Christ in His whole person."[1] And he speaks of "fixing the economy of man's salvation upon its true and proper basis, which is this: that in the sacraments we are made and continued members of Christ's body, of His flesh and of His bone. Our union with the Deity rests entirely upon our mystical union with our Lord's humanity, which is personally united with His divine nature, which is essentially united with God the Father, the head and fountain of all. So stands the economy; which shows the high importance of the principle before mentioned. And it is well that Romanists and Lutherans, and Greeks also, even the whole

---

[1] *Doctr. of the Euch.* (Oxford, 1880), p. 192. Waterland considers St. John vi. to refer to a divine gift, not exclusively but specially bestowed upon us in the eucharist.

East and West, have preserved it, and yet preserve it." [1]

It would indeed be hard for English churchmen to speak otherwise, the language of the Prayer Book being so constant and imperative as to the reality and character of the gift conveyed through the partaking of the bread and wine. But the point needs to be made emphatic, because with the holding of this doctrine, in such real sense as admits of its being deliberately and calmly stated and insisted upon, all real intellectual difficulty about the eucharist ought to be over. Beyond this we may seek to conform our apprehension and our statements as exactly as possible to the general mind of the church and the language of the New Testament, and to avoid errors and corruptions of which history warns us, but the chief point of difficulty is already past.

Both Hooker and Waterland are laying down in these passages what they conceive to be the point of agreement even among the

[1] *L.c.*, p. 520.

THE NATURE OF THE GIFT. 53

various schools of Christians who adhered to the Reformation. No doubt there were already Zwinglians or Socinians who made of the Holy Communion only a *symbolic* representation of the death of Christ and of the benefits which we receive thereby: only an occasion when we solemnly eat the broken bread and drink the outpoured wine and in connection with these speaking symbols mentally realize our union with our crucified Lord. And it does not, I suppose, admit of doubt that in the Protestant and Evangelical bodies of the Continent and of England this purely figurative view has since their day obtained the widest diffusion—as far as theory goes; though the practical devotional attitude of believers towards the sacrament has, we may well believe, habitually reached a higher level. But Hooker and Waterland could appeal, not to the Lutherans only with their (reputed) consubstantiation, but to the remodelled doctrine of Calvin, when he had separated himself from Zwingli and asserted in the strongest language the actual and substantial communication to us in the sacrament of Christ's body and blood, His life and self, to be our spiritual food.[1] This was the substantial point of agreement, as the outcome of all the controversies of the Reformation, between the divided portions of the ancient church, and nearly all the Reformed bodies.

And this belief did but carry on the tradition of the church from the days before the controversy about transubstantiation, which so painfully confused the intellectual issue. This is specially apparent in the teaching of the great theological fathers of the fourth and fifth centuries. Athanasius is set to vindicate the true godhead of Christ and the unity of His person; and thus he explains that the reason why we become partakers of the divine nature (or, as he says, "are deified") by partaking of the body of Christ, is because what we receive is not "the body of some man, but the body of the Lord Himself."[2] And in regard to the "eating

[1] See, for a collection of passages from Calvin, Paget's *Introduction to Hooker B. v.* (Clarendon Press, 1899), pp. 180 ff.

[2] *Ep.* lxi. 2 (*P. G.* xxvi. 1085).

THE NATURE OF THE GIFT. 55

Christ's flesh," according to St. John vi., he would have us remember that it is indeed the flesh that Christ was wearing of which He spoke, but that flesh as spiritualized and raised to the heavenly region, and therefore to be not "corporally" but spiritually conceived, as it is also for a spiritual nourishment that it is distributed.[1] It is plain what Athanasius' belief was both as to the reality and as to the spirituality of the eucharistic gift; as to its being truly the body and the blood, but the body and the blood of the whole living and divine person, spiritually conceived and spiritually imparted.

These points are repeatedly asserted by Cyril of Alexandria.[2] "When we celebrate the bloodless worship in our churches and approach the mystic gifts, and are sanctified by becoming partakers of the holy flesh and the precious blood of our common Saviour Christ, it is not as common flesh that we

---

[1] *Ep. ad Serap.* iv. 19 (*P. G.* xxvi. 665). I have given the passage in *Dissertations*, p. 305.

[2] See *Dissert.* p. 306, and *Ep.* xvii. (*ad Nest*) *P. G.* lxxvii. 113. I have used compression in translating.

receive it, God forbid! or as the flesh of a man in however close relation to God: it is as being truly life-giving flesh that we receive it, because it is His own flesh who is the Word and Himself the Life." Or again, "We receive within us the Word of the Father, incarnate for our sakes, and both life and life-giving."[1]

The same thoughts and arguments are familiar in the western fathers, Hilary and Augustine.[2] And when Leo is emphasizing the counter aspect of the truth about our Lord to that which had occupied Athanasius and Cyril—when he is emphasizing the permanence and reality of our Lord's manhood,—there is still an argument to be drawn from the familiar belief in the eucharist. "Can they," that is his opponents, he asks, "lie in such depths of ignorance as not even to have heard of what is so familiar in every one's mouth in the church of God, that not even infants' lips are silent about the truth of the body and blood of Christ in the sacraments

---

[1] *In Luc.* lxxii. 19, *P. G.* lxxii. 908.
[2] See *Dissert.* p. 306.

THE NATURE OF THE GIFT. 57

of communion ? For this is what is given, this is what is taken, in that mystical distribution of spiritual sustenance; that receiving the virtue of the heavenly food, we should pass into His flesh who was made our flesh."[1]

I will make only one more quotation from a theologian of this period—St. Cyril of Jerusalem (c. 345). "Therefore," he says, "with full assurance let us partake of the bread and wine as being the body and blood of Christ. For in the figure of bread is given thee the body, and in the figure of wine is given thee the blood, in order that by partaking of the body and the blood thou mayest become of one body and one blood with Him. For it is thus also we become Christ-bearers, His body and His blood being distributed over our limbs.[2] Thus, according to blessed Peter, we become partakers of the divine nature."

This same belief (only, as would be

[1] *Ep.* lix. 2; *cf. serm.* xci. 3 (*P. L.* liv. 452, 868).

[2] Or "having received of His body and blood into our members." *Catech.* xxii. 3. See, on reading and meaning, Dr. Gifford in *Nicene and Ante-Nicene Fathers*, Cyril of Jerusalem, pp. xxxvii. ff.; and below, p. 63.

expected, less explicitly stated) runs back to the beginning,[1] with certain exceptions, to be mentioned directly. It is heard first of all, outside the New Testament, in Ignatius of Antioch. "The false teachers [who denied the reality of our Lord's manhood] abstain from eucharist and prayer because they do not acknowledge that the eucharist is the flesh of our Saviour Jesus Christ, which suffered for our sins, which by His goodness the Father raised up." "Take care then to frequent but one eucharist (*i.e.*, to avoid schism); for there is one flesh of our Lord Jesus Christ and one cup for unity in His blood; one altar, as there is one bishop with the presbyters and deacons." "Breaking one bread, which is the medicine of immortality, the antidote that we should not die, but live in Christ Jesus for ever."[2]

This is really, then, the catholic faith about the eucharistic gift — so much so that Thomassin, a theologian who has the widest and profoundest knowledge of the

[1] Cyprian *de domin. orat.* 18 is very explicit.
[2] On Ignatius see app. note 4, p. 292.

THE NATURE OF THE GIFT.

fathers, can find no other phrase to summarize his massive quotations from them on the subject than by speaking of the eucharist as " the extension of the incarnation"—the instrument for extending the incarnate life. " The incarnation," he says, " gaped, as it were, incomplete and suspended, until in all its parts and elements it was fulfilled through the eucharist." [1]

But there are three modifications which must be given to any statement as to the catholicity of this faith, before it can be regarded as approximately complete.

(1) There was a tendency in the earlier school of Alexandria, by a process of intellectual refinement, to explain—I must say to explain away—the body (or flesh) and blood of Christ as meaning no more than His word or His spirit; and thus even to make the eucharist not much more than an occasion for mystical contemplation. This tendency was really influential, and not heretical or schismatical, for it clung to,

---

[1] Thomassin *Theol. Dogm.* "De Incarn." lib. x. cap. xxii. § 4.

even while for its own purpose it refined upon, the common belief and the common worship. But it came to be judged, and surely with justice, as an inadequate mode of belief. For it is not merely the Spirit for our spirits, or the teaching for our intellects, that we ask for and receive, but the whole Christ for our whole selves.[1] Nothing less than this, as we have already seen, can satisfy the language of the New Testament.

(2) There is a sporadic tendency—as in Clement of Alexandria, Jerome, Ratramn and some of his contemporaries,[2] in our

[1] For Origen's own tendency of belief the clearest passages are *in Matt. comment. ser.* 82, 85; *in Johan.* xxxii. 16; *cf.* Bigg *Christian Platonists* (Oxford, 1886), pp. 219—222. He witnesses that his was not the common faith: "Let the bread and the cup be conceived by the simple according to the commoner acceptation of the eucharist; but by those who have learnt to hear with a deeper ear, according to the divine promise, even that of the nourishing word of the truth." In fact Origen's depreciation of the "flesh" goes with his depreciation of the historical sense. It is part of his allegorism. The tendency described above mostly accompanies, whether as cause or effect, the misunderstanding of St. John vi. 62. See app. note 2, p. 290.

[2] Quoted in *Dissertations*, p. 239.

THE NATURE OF THE GIFT.

own English Aelfric (probably taught by Ratramn) and in some later Anglicans, such as John Johnson—to distinguish the eucharistic body and blood of Christ from that in which He was born and suffered and died, as being "spiritual," and not "natural" or "real," and thus a different body. The exact meaning of this language is not always easy to fix. But (except perhaps in the case of Clement, who would be under the same influences as Origen) what they mean is only what has been expressed, and better expressed, by Athanasius and the church generally, in saying that the eucharistic body and blood are the very body and blood in which Christ lived and died *and rose and ascended*, only bestowed on us in a spiritual and heavenly manner; the same body, only not now in its material particles, but in its spiritual principle and virtue. This, I say, is a better mode of statement than that which speaks of different bodies or different kinds of blood, because St. John vi. would plainly intimate to us that that with which we are fed as the bread of life is nothing else than what Christ is—Himself in His manhood glorified.

"In the explication of this question," says Jeremy Taylor, "it is much insisted upon that it be enquired whether, when we say we believe Christ's body to be 'really' in the sacrament, we mean, that body, that flesh, that was born of the Virgin Mary, that was crucified, dead and buried. I answer, I know none else that He had or hath: there is but one body of Christ natural and glorified; but he that says that body is glorified that was crucified, says it is the same body, but not after the same manner; and so it is in the sacrament; we eat and drink the body and blood of Christ that was broken and poured forth: for there is no other body, no other blood of Christ; but though it is the same which we eat and drink, yet it is in another manner."[1]

(3) There was an early tendency—opposite to that of the Alexandrians—

[1] Jer. Taylor, *Real Presence*, § 1, 11.

apparent in Irenæus and, somewhat differently, in Tertullian, and later in Cyril of Jerusalem and more plainly in Gregory of Nyssa,[1] to lay a one-sided emphasis on the idea that the eucharist was given to cleanse our *bodies* and nourish them for the life immortal: it was to impart the "antidote of immortality" to the perishing flesh. Pursuing this line of thinking, the fathers mentioned above seem to identify the body and blood of Christ with the bread and wine considered as physical food. These, as enriched by the divine Word or Spirit with life-giving powers, are called, and indeed become, Christ's body and blood (Gregory postulates even a physical change in the elements), and, as eaten or drunken, nourish the human body with an immortal life and divine fellowship with God. It would be unjust to commit men, who

[1] For Irenæus see *c. hær.*, iv. 18, 5, v. 2, 3. On Tertullian see *Dissertations*, pp. 308 ff. On Cyril see above, p. 57, and Gifford's note referred to; also *Cat.* xxii. 5. For Gregory *Cat. Mag.* 37. Gregory makes baptism with faith the salvation of the soul, and the communion of the body and blood the salvation of the body.

were making the first attempt to express mysterious truth, to all that their words sometimes seem to imply. Indeed the first use of theological language on any subject, before it has been rigorously cross-questioned from outside, is, except in the case of the specially inspired authors, very seldom accurate. But the tendency we have been describing naturally makes these fathers think of the eucharistic gift almost exclusively as a bodily gift—a gift of body for body, without thought for the wholeness of Christ's person; and represents therefore a divergent tendency, similar to what has been noticed in the Alexandrians though in the opposite direction, and, like theirs, on maturer reflection unacceptable.

For though in the Holy Communion our body is sanctified through the sanctification of our spirit, and transformed and endowed, in subtle and secret ways which pass our comprehension, with capacity for the life immortal; yet it is through the spirit and not directly. Primarily the gift of Christ's body and blood is a spiritual gift for the

THE NATURE OF THE GIFT.

spirit. Faith alone is the instrument which can receive it, and not the mouth of the body. The gift accompanies the material bread and wine, but is to be distinguished from it. And inasmuch as the body and blood are spiritual, they are indistinguishable or inseparable from the living person, the whole Christ. "He that eateth me, even he shall live by me."

Already we shall have seen that it was no easy matter for the church to express its common faith and feeling about the eucharist in intellectual formulas. There were more or less marked divergent theological tendencies—though there was little consciousness of their divergence—especially in the second and third centuries. But the only formulas in which the faith of the church in general could ever find adequate expression are such as declare that the gift communicated to us in the eucharistic feast is verily and indeed that of the flesh or body and blood of Christ according to a spiritual and heavenly manner; that is to say the gift of Christ Himself, in His whole person, given to us for the sanctification of our whole persons, that He may dwell in us and we in Him.

It stands to reason that if there be thus, as the Christian church so constantly believed, a real communication to us of the flesh and blood of Christ, it must be the "flesh" and "blood" of the glorified Christ, for no other exists. These mysterious things are given to us in the eucharist under conditions which recall a past state—the state of sacrificial death. It is our Lord as dying that faith recalls: it is His death for us that we "proclaim till He come"[1] in the breaking of the bread. But those very words of St. Paul, "till He come," suggest that He is no longer dead, that He is alive and in heaven. The person who now feeds us with His own very life, divine and human, is He who is set before us in a vision of the Apocalypse as a "Lamb as it had been slain," but alive for evermore in the heavenly places.[2]

[1] 1 Cor. xi. 26.
[2] See below also, p. 181.

THE NATURE OF THE GIFT.

There is only one other point that needs touching upon at this stage of the argument, and that is the special sense in which this gift is connected with the *eucharist*. It may be said—What does this eating the flesh of Christ and drinking His blood mean that is not meant also by being baptized "into Christ" and being "His members"? You would admit that this eating does not mean a consuming of any material atoms or elements of Christ's body: it means absorbing the spiritual forces of His humanity: but this is what is also meant by membership of Christ. Do we not, therefore, in the true sense eat Christ's flesh and drink Christ's blood also in baptism?

This question is not sufficiently answered with the simple negative. When Fulgentius of Ruspe (A.D. 507) was confronted with the question how, if the eating of Christ's flesh and drinking His blood was necessary to eternal life, could a baptized person, who without fault of his own had died after baptism without having received the Holy Communion, obtain salvation, he gave the not perhaps very adequate answer, that such an one had already eaten Christ's flesh and drunk His blood by the very fact of becoming a member of His body; and he claimed for this answer the authority of "the fathers," and especially of St. Augustine.[1] The answer is not morally adequate, for it fails to recognize that God is free to give His gifts of spiritual life to all "men of good will," apart from any sacraments; but it suggests an element of truth which it is important to acknowledge. It is one and the same spiritual process which is described as being made a member of Christ or being baptized into Christ, and also as eating His flesh and drinking His blood: it is one and the same process which is described as being regenerated by the Spirit in baptism and as receiving Him in confirmation. And the process is

[1] *Ep.* xii. 24—26 (*P. L.* lxv. 590—592). St. Augustine in the passage he quotes does not do more than indirectly imply the answer; but it is more clearly implied in the language used by him and by Pope Innocent: see Aug. *Epp.* clxxxvi. 28—29, clxxxii. 5; and also a citation from Augustine, on Bede's authority, in Thomas Aq. *S. Th.* p. iii. qu. 73, 3.

THE NATURE OF THE GIFT. 69

a vital thing, which cannot be wholly sundered into parts, and in which we cannot draw sharp lines. We cannot say simply that the inward gift of the eucharist (or of confirmation) is *not* given in baptism.[1] What we can say is that the fellowship in the ever-continuous supply of the new life is, for the needs of our nature, given to us in stages and by degrees of growing intensity and power; and that each stage of the communication is identified with a separate sacrament which is thus positively characterized only in a certain way.

Thus baptism is our regeneration, or our incorporation into the new manhood by the Spirit, and involves that deep breach with the past which is expressed by the forgiveness of sins: confirmation is the bestowal of the unction of the Holy Spirit of Christ for the full equipment of the personal life, both for individual strength and social service: the

[1] Except indeed by using the negative, as it is often used in Scripture, when what is exactly meant is "not to the same degree," or "not in the same sense." This use of the negative is admirably noted and explained by Berengar. See *Dissertations*, p. 257.

eucharist is the full and repeated communion in His all-powerful manhood—the eating His flesh and drinking His blood—and through His manhood, the perfect communion with God. Throughout it is the same gift, ministered by the same Spirit: but it is the same gift in different stages of completeness: and it is the completest degree of participation in Christ's manhood which, in the language of the New Testament, is identified with Holy Communion. This is the truth which was expressed by the African Christians when they called baptism " salvation " and the eucharist " life." [1]

[1] See Augustin *de pecc. mer. et rem.* i. 34.

§ 2. *The relation of the spiritual gift to the bread and wine.*

But if the gift given in Holy Communion is continuous with that given in baptism and cannot be sharply separated from it, how is it with the outward and visible sign or sacramental channel? In baptism the spiritual gift is attached to an *act* of bathing or washing defined by certain accompanying words.[1] In the "breaking of the bread" is the spiritual gift merely, in the same way, attached to the act or process of eating and drinking?

Such has certainly not been the mind of the church from the first. It has believed that, by consecration of the portions of bread and wine which have been solemnly

---

[1] This is the meaning of the technical word "form" applied by theologians to the sacred sacramental words. They define or give form to the "matter" of an external action which in itself is quite vague in its significance.

set apart or offered, the spiritual gift of Christ's body and blood is, in some way, attached to these elements (however the relationship is to be described) before they are eaten and drunken, and independently of such eating and drinking. As Dr. Mozley says—and he was not a thinker who would be prone to exaggerate this aspect of the question—" Certainly the ground taken by the early church with respect to the spiritual part of the sacrament of the Lord's Supper—the body and blood of our Lord—was *not* that that spiritual part was only an internal matter, a moral effect of the act of participation upon the mind. The Lord's body and blood was regarded as a reality external to the mind, even as the bread and wine was; it was considered as joined to the bread and wine, and so existing with it in one sacrament. 'The eating and drinking of it in the sacrament,' Thorndike says, 'presupposes the being of it in the sacrament . . . unless a man can spiritually eat the flesh and blood of Christ in and by the sacrament, which is not in the sacrament

THE OBJECTIVE PRESENCE. 73

when he eats and drinks it, but by his eating and drinking of it comes to be there.' The language of the early church on the subject is so well known, and so large a body of it meets us in the writings of the early ages, that we need not dwell long upon this characteristic of early teaching on the subject of the eucharist."[1]

Dr. Mozley proceeds to modify this statement by a counter-statement, that as the gift was a spiritual gift, so faith only could recognize or receive it. Some such counter-statement—some statement of the "relativity" of the presence—is most necessary, and will give us matter for serious consideration. But for the present we are concerned only with part of the question— the consecration of the elements themselves to become sacramentally identified with the body and blood of Christ.

This is what is called the doctrine of an *objectively* real presence in the eucharist. Of course this phrase might express equally well the reality of the spiritual grace imparted

[1] *Lectures and Theol. Papers* (Longmans), p. 202.

in baptism. For that too is objective; in the sense that it is not the product of the receiver's mind, but is a real gift from God, given and received; and that it must be conceived as given irrespective of the state of mind or condition of faith of the receiver; so that an unconscious infant is regenerated, and even a bad man really receives the spiritual endowment of his nature which he only ignores, or misuses to his greater hurt. In this sense all who are sacramental believers would admit the gift in the holy eucharist to be objective—that is, to be a real divine gift communicated in the act of eating and drinking. The word however is generally used in a further sense in which it is not applicable to baptism; and its use in this sense is so valuable for purposes of distinction that it had better be retained. It expresses the belief that prior to reception, and independently of the faith of the individual, the body and blood of Christ are made present "under the forms of" bread and wine, or in some real though undefined way identified with them.

That this was the belief of the early church generally, as Dr. Mozley asserts, may be shown by evidence of three kinds.

I. There is the evidence of the reverence displayed towards the consecrated elements —not in the way of what is now called eucharistic worship, as of the divine Christ present under the forms of bread and wine, of which, as will appear, the evidence is ambiguous; but of scrupulous care that no fragment of the consecrated bread or drop of the wine should fall. There is very early evidence[1] of such care from Alexandria, Africa, Jerusalem, and perhaps Rome: so that it must represent an universal and primitive Christian tradition of reverence. Now it has nothing corresponding to it in the case of the water of baptism. Indeed an early method was to baptize in running water. This is important, because occasionally the language of early Christian writers about the consecration of the water in baptism, or of the chrism, would suggest that the water or oil itself

[1] See app. note 5, p. 293.

was changed.[1] But (to go no farther) the difference between the treatment of the water or oil and the treatment of the bread and wine points to a difference in what was believed with regard to them: it indicates that the particular portions of bread and wine consecrated were regarded as having become in themselves holy and sacred things.

II. The language of the eucharistic consecration explains this belief. What we may call the normal form of consecration consists of three parts: there is (*a*) the recitation of the narrative of the institution, including the words which in the West have come to be recognized as the instrument of consecration, but which originally only formed a part of the great " giving of thanks," the solemn commemoration of the divine glory and goodness as shown in nature and in the whole history of redemption, and specially in the passion and death of our Lord, and in His institution of the eucharist in remembrance of Himself. Next (*b*) there is a

[1] This identity of phraseology has been much exaggerated: see app. note 6, p. 294.

THE OBJECTIVE PRESENCE. 77

solemn oblation of the elements in accordance with Christ's institution—"wherefore we, remembering His passion, death and resurrection, etc., here offer and present." Thirdly (c) there is an invocation of the Holy Ghost, a prayer that God would send down the Holy Ghost—whose special function it is to communicate the life of Christ to the church[1]—to make the elements to be the body and blood of Christ for the reception of the faithful. Here is a specimen of such a consecration prayer from the directory of worship known as the Apostolical Constitutions.

(a) "Calling therefore to remembrance those things which He endured for our sakes,

[1] This scriptural principle explains the instinct of the church to invoke the Holy Ghost upon the elements. Thus St. Cyril finds in the eucharistic invocation an instance of the general principle that "every grace and every perfect gift comes upon us from the Father through the Son by the Holy Ghost" (*in Luc.* xxii. 19). See E. S. Ffoulkes *Primitive Consecration of the Eucharistic Oblation* (Hayes, 1885), pp. 13 ff. Mr. Ffoulkes is right at any rate in his contention that the church for many centuries both in East and West attributed the consecration of the elements to the action of the Holy Ghost invoked by the church.

we give thanks unto Thee, O God Almighty, not as we ought, but as we are able, and fulfil His institution. For in the same night that He was betrayed, taking bread into His holy and immaculate hands, and looking up to Thee, His God and Father, and breaking it, He gave it to His disciples, saying, This is the mystery of the New Testament; take of it; eat; this is My body, which is broken for many for the remission of sins. Likewise, also, having mingled the cup with wine and water, and blessed it, He gave it to them, saying, Drink ye all of it; this is My blood which is shed for many for the remission of sins; do this in remembrance of Me, for as often as ye eat of this bread, and drink of this cup, ye do shew forth My death till I come.

(*b*) " Wherefore having in remembrance His passion, death, and resurrection from the dead, His return into heaven, and His future second appearance, when He shall come with glory and power to judge the quick and the dead, and to render to every man according to his works: we offer to

THE OBJECTIVE PRESENCE. 79

Thee, our King and our God, according to His institution, this bread and this cup, giving thanks to Thee through Him, that Thou hast thought us worthy to stand before Thee, and to serve as priests unto Thee.

(c) "And we beseech Thee that Thou wilt look graciously on these gifts now lying before Thee, O Thou all-sufficient God, and accept them to the honour of Thy Christ; and send down Thy Holy Spirit, the witness of the sufferings of the Lord Jesus, on this sacrifice, that He may make[1] this bread the body of Thy Christ, and this cup the blood of Thy Christ, that all who shall partake of it may be confirmed in godliness, may receive remission of their sins, may be delivered from the devil and his wiles, may be

[1] Or "declare" (ἀποφήνῃ). This word, with the similar ἀπυδεικνύναι (or ἀναδεικνύναι), is sometimes used indistinguishably from ποιεῖν, "to make to be." But as used in the liturgies it carries with it probably not only the idea of making the elements to be what they were not before, but also the idea of revealing or declaring what they have become to the faithful. " He shall take of mine, and shall declare it unto you." Ποιεῖν, ἀποδεικνύναι, ἀναδεικνύναι are all found in the eucharistic invocation, and the language of the fathers in describing it, more or less indiscriminately.

filled with the Holy Ghost, may be made worthy of Thy Christ, and may obtain everlasting life, Thou, O Lord Almighty, being reconciled unto them."

This is from an ideal rather than an historical rite, but it is typical or representative of the form common to the Greek liturgies, which must go back along many lines to very early days. It is just such a form that St. Basil regards as derived from the apostles by unwritten tradition.[1]

Not that it is in all its parts to be regarded as essential or universal. Thus—

(1) St. Cyril of Jerusalem in his detailed account of the liturgy[2] of his church and age is strikingly silent about any commemorative recitation of the "words of institution"; and this at least shows, what he elsewhere makes plain, that he did not attribute importance to them as a necessary part of the form of consecration.

(2) There is not always explicit mention

---

[1] *De Spir. Sanct.* 66.

[2] *Cat.* xxiii. 7; *cf.* Brightman *Liturgies* (Oxford, 1896), p. 469.

of the Holy Ghost. Thus in the prayers for the eucharist ascribed to Bishop Serapion (c. 350) the invocation is, "O God of Truth, let *Thy holy Word* come down upon this bread, that the bread may become the body of the Word, and upon this cup, that the cup may become the blood of the Truth; and make all who communicate to receive the medicine of life for the healing of all sickness and the strengthening of all progress and virtue."[1] We know that such a form was exceptional, and that the Holy Ghost was generally invoked in Egypt in the fourth century;[2] but in earlier days—in Irenæus' time (c. 180)—all we can be sure of is that there was some invocation of God to act in His divine power upon the oblations. "The bread from the earth," says Irenæus, "receiving the invocation of God is no longer

---

[1] *Journal of Theol. Stud.*, Oct. 1899, p. 106. Previously there is a prayer: "Fill this sacrifice, O Lord, with Thy power and the participation of Thee, for we have offered Thee this living sacrifice, this bloodless offering."

[2] See the language of Peter of Alexandria, Athanasius' successor, in Theodoret *E. H.* iv. 19; and of St. Theophilus in Jerome *Ep.* xcviii. 13.

common bread but eucharist, made up of two realities (things), an earthly and a heavenly"; and twice elsewhere, "The bread and the mixed cup, receiving upon themselves the word of God, become eucharist, that is the body and blood of Christ."[1]

(3) The prayer was not always explicit as to what was the effect desired by consecration. Thus the "anaphora" or prayer of oblation, of the Ethiopic Church, which appears to be very ancient, runs: "We beseech Thee that Thou wouldest send Thine Holy Spirit on the oblation of this church: give it unto all them that partake together for sanctification and for fulfilling with the Holy Ghost and for confirming true faith."[2] And in the Gallican rites (which, whatever their origin, represent the worship of the greater part of the West for a long period, at least from the fourth century) the invoca-

---

[1] *C. haer.* iv. 18. 5, v. 2, 3: see app. note 7, p. 295.

[2] Brightman *l.c.* p. 190 (*cf.* p. 287). Just below, after invocation, occurs a prayer for those who receive " of the holy mystery of the body and blood of Christ the Almighty Lord our God," p. 191.

THE OBJECTIVE PRESENCE.

tion-prayer is equally vague: "We pray Thee that Thou wouldest bless with Thy benediction this sacrifice, and water it with the dew of Thy Holy Spirit, that it may be to all those who receive it a legitimate eucharist."[1] This vague phrase is described by Duchesne as "characteristic" of the Gallican rites. But there is no doubt that the Gallican or Spanish writers of the period to which it belongs would have interpreted it precisely in the sense of the more explicit Greek prayers. Their belief did not fall below that of St. Ambrose of Milan, who speaks of the "sacraments" or sacramental elements as being "by the mysterious action of the sacred prayer [elsewhere described as an invocation of the Holy Ghost] transfigured into the flesh and blood of the Lord."[2]

(4) The Roman canon stands apart in having, or having had, no invocation. In Africa there is evidence that the Holy Spirit

---

[1] Neale and Forbes' *Ancient Lit.* pp. 4, 11, 15, etc. Duchesne *Origines du Culte Chrétien*, Paris, 1895, p. 208.

[2] *De fide* iv. 124, *de S. S.* iii. 114.

was formally invoked, for Optatus of Milevis (c. 368) speaks of the altars as places "where God Almighty is invoked; where the Holy Spirit descends at the church's prayer," and afterwards as "the seat of the body and blood of Christ."[1] Now Africa got its ecclesiastical system from Rome, and it is therefore, as well as for other reasons, probable that the same was the case in the early Roman church. But when the fixed Roman canon was framed in Latin (possibly in the fourth century), the place commonly occupied by the invocation of the Holy Spirit was taken by the prayer " that the oblations might be carried by the hand of God's holy angel to the heavenly altar, in the sight of His divine majesty, that as many as received by participation from the altar the holy body and blood of His Son, might be filled with all heavenly grace."[2] In the canon indeed as it exists at present there is at an earlier

---

[1] *De schism. Don.* vi. 1., *P. L.* xi. 1065.

[2] There is a somewhat similar prayer in the Clementine liturgy and in the liturgies of St. James and St. Chrysostom, but after, and independently of, the invocation or consecra-

THE OBJECTIVE PRESENCE. 85

point the prayer "that this oblation may *become to us* the body and blood of Thy dearly beloved Son": but it does not belong to its original form.[1]

In the church of Rome then a prayer, couched in rather imaginative language, for the carrying up of the earthly elements to the heavenly altar to be returned to earth again as the life-giving body and blood, takes the place of the normal prayer for the descent of the Holy Spirit to consecrate the elements visibly lying on the earthly altar. And there is, consequently, much less emphasis in the original Roman canon on what the elements become by consecration, apart from reception. Meanwhile however the teaching at Rome was not uncertain. "The elements," writes Gelasius[2] (A.D. 480),

tion : see Brightman *op. cit.* pp. 23, 58, 390. The right interpretation of the prayer in the Roman canon is very uncertain.

[1] *I.e.* as quoted in the *de sacramentis*, see Duchesne *op. cit.* p. 170.

[2] See quotation in *Dissert.* p. 275, and *cf.* the phrase in the Leonine Sacramentary (Christmas mass, *P. L.* lv. 147): "By the operation of the Holy Ghost, our sacrifice is now the body and blood of the Priest Himself."

"pass into the divine substance by the action of the Holy Spirit, remaining at the same time in the propriety of their own nature." And this Roman substitute for the invocation is isolated and exceptional. The invocation of the Holy Spirit or of the divine power upon the elements, *to make them Christ's body and blood in order that they might be received by the worshippers to their spiritual profit*, was the earlier form, and best represents the earlier teaching. Certain evidence of this lies in the statements, anterior to any of the liturgical documents, of the fathers of the second century — Justin and Irenæus — already quoted.[1] And I will add the witness of Origen: "Let Celsus, then, who knows not God, render his thank-offerings to demons; while we, giving thanks to the maker of the universe, eat also, with thanksgiving and prayer over what has been given us, our oblations of bread, which on account of the prayer become a certain holy body that also makes those holy who partake of it with a sound disposition."[2]

[1] See pp. 6 ff, 81 f. [2] *C. Cels.* viii. 33.

THE OBJECTIVE PRESENCE.

III. We may further illustrate the belief of the ancient church in the objectivity of the eucharistic gift by the language of theologians. Justin, Irenæus and Origen have been already cited to prove that in the second and third centuries the bread and wine were believed to become by consecration —for the reception of the faithful, no doubt, but yet in themselves to become—the body and blood of Christ. And in the fourth century this belief gains more abundant expression.

It is chiefly among the Greeks however that a strong devotional enthusiasm developed itself for the eucharist, such as is apparent in St. Cyril of Jerusalem's lectures on the mysteries, and in St. Chrysostom's sermons and writings. The special purpose for which the sacred presence is given—sacramental communion—is always full in view; indeed, Chrysostom, as is well known, strongly protested against Christians being present without communicating. But before communion, through the consecrating action of the Holy Spirit upon the bread and wine, of which these fathers speak with such rapt devotion, Christ's body and His blood become present, and Christ Himself is there, our high-priest, our king, and our sacrifice, in the midst of the worshipping church. Occasionally this presence is spoken of in language which represents precisely the modern phrase—"the whole Christ made present in" or "under the form of bread and wine";[1] as when Cyril speaks of the communicant "receiving the King in his right hand";[2] or when Chrysostom speaks of the priest "continuously manipulating the common Lord of all," and of "Him who sits with the Father, giving Himself to be held in the hands of all."[3] But more often the language is such as is suggested by the words "symbol" or "type."

[1] See Pusey *Real Presence from the Fathers* (Parker, 1855), pp. 131 ff.: "The term 'in' as used by the Fathers does not express any local inclusion of the body and blood of Christ; it denotes their presence there after the manner of a sacrament." He compares "Christ dwells *in* our hearts by faith," "God dwelleth *in* us," "the Holy Spirit dwelleth *in* us," none of these phrases expressing local inclusion.

[2] *Cat.* xxiii. 21.

[3] *De sacerdot.* iii. 4, vi. 4 (*P. G.* xlvii. 642, 681).

"What is nowadays understood by 'symbol,'" says Harnack, "is a thing which is not that which it represents; at that time [*i.e.*, the early Christian centuries] symbol denoted a thing which, in some kind of sense, really is what it signifies; but, on the other hand, according to the ideas of the period, the really heavenly element lay either in or behind the visible form without investing itself with it. Accordingly the *distinction* of a symbolic from a realistic conception of the Supper is altogether to be rejected."[1]

The symbol, or "outward and visible sign," then, is the evidence to the senses of a divine reality actually present. It is for this reason that the visible gifts and altar are called "mystical" or "spiritual." For as surely as with the outward eye you behold the bread and wine lying on the table, so

[1] Harnack *Lehrbuch der Dogmeng.* i. p. 360 [Eng. trans. (Williams and Norgate) ii. p. 144—in this case not quite trustworthy]; *cf.* i. p. 149: "The symbolic for that period is not to be thought of as the opposite of the objective or the real: but it is the mysterious and divinely-enwrought, which stands out against the natural or profanely clear."

surely with the eye of faith you are to behold heaven opened and brought down to earth, and the angels worshipping, and the eternal living priest exhibiting to you His once offered sacrifice in His body and His blood, and coming to you to feed you with the life-giving food. Certainly the theologians of that period, though they are highly rhetorical and occasionally use language which could not be rigidly justified, as a whole suggest to us not precisely an image of a Christ *contained in* or *under veils of* bread and wine. There can be no doubt that their theology led them to shrink from any such formulation of their belief as suggested a Christ subjecting Himself to limits of space. They preferred the language which suggests the breaking away of material limits before the eye of faith. Thus, when Gregory of Nyssa, in discouraging people from going on pilgrimages, suggests that their own land is thicker than Palestine with holy places, because it has so many more altars "by means of which our Lord's name is glorified"; the phrase which the eucharistic altar

THE OBJECTIVE PRESENCE.

suggests to him is that of "inferring God's presence from visible symbols."[1]

I do not think it can be denied that these fathers would have shrunk from any formulated teaching of "Christ made present on the altar under the forms of bread and wine." They would rather say "The bread and wine are types of spiritual realities really present. As surely as you see the consecration of the elements by the human priest with your outward eyes, so surely with the eye of faith you are to see the divine Christ present amid the worshipping angels, Himself the consecrating priest[2] as Himself the sacrifice — present to feed you with the spiritual food of His body and blood in the earthly food of bread and wine."

It is a suggestive fact that they frequently introduce into the immediate neighbourhood of some particularly definite or local phrase with reference to our Lord's eucharistic presence, another of a vague character which takes the edge off the seemingly

[1] *De peregin.* (*P. G.* xlvi. 1012).
[2] On this point Chrysostom and others continually insist.

local definition. Optatus, the African, for example, when protesting against the violation by the Donatists of catholic altars, speaks of them, in a phrase already quoted, as " the seat of the body and blood of Christ," " where His body and His blood used to dwell for certain moments of time." But in the immediate context he adds, " whereon the prayers of the people and the members of Christ are borne,"[1] which destroys the exactness of the previous phrases, for the "members of Christ" (the church) do not, in any local sense, lie upon the altar any more than their prayers. Or again, when Chrysostom has told the people that they can see Christ on the altar, as the Magi saw Him in the manger, that " here, too, will the Lord's body lie "—he adds, "not wrapped in swaddling clothes, but encircled all round by the Holy Ghost;" and goes on to speak of the altar as "full of spiritual fire," like a fountain of flame. "Do not therefore approach it with straw or wood or hay, lest the conflagration become greater

[1] Optatus *de schism. Don.* vi. 1. (*P. L.* xi. 1065—6).

and consume the soul which partakes."[1] In this way they habitually blunt the edge of their more definite or quasi-local expressions about the eucharistic presence.

Now it has been a matter of general agreement even in the later western church that the presence of Christ in the eucharist is not really local. "Our Lord," wrote Cardinal Newman, "neither descends from heaven upon our altars, nor moves when carried in procession. The visible species change their position, but He does not move."[2] But there has often been very considerable need to carry out this admission of theologians into the current and popular teaching of the church. And the fathers, who were popular teachers, may be our guides in doing this. They escaped the perils of localization by a rich variety of language.

But I do not think it is disputable that the church from the beginning did, as a whole, believe that the eucharistic elements

---

[1] Chrys. *de beat. Philog.* 3, 4 (*P. G.* xlvii. 753, 756).
[2] See *Via Media* (Pickering, 1887), ii. p. 220.

themselves in some real sense became by consecration, and prior to reception, the body and blood of Christ in the midst of the worshipping assembly; and that the body and blood thus made present objectively, in undefinable identification with the bread and wine, were the same body (or flesh) and blood as the faithful hoped to receive—that is, the flesh and blood of the living and glorified Christ, the flesh and blood which are spirit and life, and are quite inseparable from the living person of Christ Himself.

Nor does it seem to me difficult to suggest a reason, both practical and spiritual, why, if the loving purpose of Christ was to communicate to us the spiritual food of His most blessed body and blood, He should, on the institution of His sacrament, have vouchsafed the gift, first of all, as an objective presence in the church, and not conveyed it directly to the individual worshippers in connection with an act of eating bread and drinking wine. For even if the members of the church ate and drank

THE OBJECTIVE PRESENCE. 95

all together at the same meal, yet the act of eating is separate to each individual, and the divine gift would thus have taken the character of an individual communication. But the presence vouchsafed amongst them emphasizes unity; as apparently the divine Spirit on the Day of Pentecost, when He came to make the church one, symbolized His coming in a fire which appeared first as one and then divided and distributed itself in fiery tongues.[1] In each case that which was to be distributed to all was given first as one object, to make evident the unity and unifying effect of the divine gift.[2]

So can we give its most natural force to the language of St. Paul about the one loaf making us as we partake of it one body, because breaking and eating the bread we are partaking of Christ's body, as also drinking of the cup we are partaking of His blood.[3] So, again, can we most naturally interpret the words of Ignatius already

---

[1] Acts ii. 3: "There appeared to them tongues like as of fire, dividing (or R. V. marg. 'distributing'), themselves."

[2] See app. note 8, p. 296. [3] 1 Cor. x. 16, 17.

referred to, and all the stream of Christian language which has flowed out of those words, "There is one flesh of our Lord Jesus Christ and one cup for unity in His blood."

But, reserving for the present the indisputable fact that the objective presence was given, not absolutely, but for the church and for the purpose of communion, even so there are objections to the doctrine just stated which demand consideration.

(1) The doctrine was not quite universal. The practical, devotional, attitude, we may say, was universal, but there are doctrinal explanations of particular fathers or schools of theologians of a divergent kind. I leave out of sight that somewhat mysterious document, the *Didache*,[1] because, so far as appears on the surface of that primitive manual, the eucharist is simply a social meal, touched with a certain breath of mysticism, but no more. The familiar language about the body or flesh and blood of Christ—the language of all the Gospels

[1] See however *The Church and the Ministry* (Longmans), app. note L., pp. 377 f.

THE OBJECTIVE PRESENCE. 97

and of St. Paul, and of the church as a whole—is not there: nor, to go farther back, is there any such teaching about Christ's person or sacrifice to be found there as would make this language intelligible. If the *Didache* is to be taken as it stands, as a more or less complete document speaking without deliberate reserve, we must suppose that it emanates from some only half-Christian community. But it need not be considered here, because what is absent from it is the whole language about the body and blood of Christ which has given its meaning to the Christian sacrament, and which comes, we believe, from our Lord's own lips. It is this language, and not anything short of this, which is the starting point of explanation.

But there are other writers, as has been already mentioned, who use the common Christian language, and yet explain it differently from the church in general. Thus some would almost have explained away "body" or "blood" into doctrine or spirit; while others, with a one-sided tendency of an opposite sort, so fastened their attention upon the divine grace communicated by the eucharist to the human body, as to think only of what is bodily or for the body in the eucharistic gifts, and almost ignored the whole Christ there present for our whole manhood; others, again, spoke of the body and blood of Christ in the eucharist as a different body to that which really exists in heaven. Now on these types of teaching something has been already said justifying their rejection. But with reference to the last it may be further pointed out that the divine presence which is bestowed upon the earthly elements at the altar—and all the advocates of this view believed in an objective presence of some sort on the altar—is bestowed simply in order that it may be received. Therefore we must never distinguish the objective presence in the elements from the gift that is communicated to us. And if the gift as received by us is the gift of the flesh and blood of the living Lord inseparable from Himself, the same must be the spiritual reality which co-exists

THE OBJECTIVE PRESENCE.

with the consecrated symbols of bread and wine.

These are discarded types of doctrine, which we may leave with the simple recognition that they existed, and were rather found inadequate than condemned as heretical.[1]

(2) More cogent than the argument derived from the exceptional positions of these theologians is the general absence of evidence in the patristic period of the later tendency to worship Christ in the sacrament.

In modern books of popular devotion, such as proceed from circles in which the doctrine of the real presence is accepted, a prominent feature is the stress laid on the worship of Christ, as, in virtue of consecration, made present upon the altar, as upon a throne. Thus going to the eucharist (apart from the question of communion) is spoken of as going to meet Jesus. He is said to be "coming" in the earlier part of the service: after consecration He has "come," and the

---

[1] It is important to remember that Origen's view at least did not claim to represent the common faith, but to be a refinement of it for select natures.

faithful must devoutly adore Him—Jesus present in His manhood but very God.

Now it is an admitted fact that this worship of Jesus in the sacrament is absent from the liturgies, almost entirely. Where it exists, and so far as it exists, (1) it certainly represents no original feature ; (2) it generally does not correspond to the requirement of modern sacramental worship. Thus it makes perhaps its first appearance in connection with the solemn "entrance" of the unconsecrated elements, which is treated as the entrance of Christ, the King of kings, into the world (and again and again " in a mystery " into the church) accompanied with the angelic hosts, to be offered and to become the food of the faithful ;[1] and the bread and wine are accordingly hailed already at their entrance as the body and blood of Christ.[2] Or again, in the present Mozarabic liturgy, just before the act of consecration there is a

[1] Lit. of St. James, Brightman, p. 41.

[2] Brightman, p. 267: "The body of Christ and His precious blood are upon the holy altar" (Nestorian); *cf.*, for the Gallican rites, *P. L.* lxii. 92, 93, and Duchesne, p. 195.

prayer to Christ to be present as among His disciples in the upper chamber, and Himself to consecrate the gifts.[1] Or Pope Sergius (c. 700) introduces the *Agnus Dei*, the appeal to Christ, as Lamb of God, in connection with the " breaking of the bread " just before communion.[2] But these acts of worship addressed to Christ are not to the point. Even the *Agnus Dei*, which is comparatively late, does not immediately follow the consecration. And when these are set aside there is very little left, and certainly nothing original.[3]

Thus, whatever unimportant exceptions are to be allowed, the main fact is unmistakable. The structure of the liturgy represents first a great act of worship and sacrifice—a sacrifice of praise made in connection with visible gifts of bread and wine—offered to the

[1] "Adesto, adesto, Jesu bone pontifex." *P. L.* lxxxv. 550.

[2] See Duchesne *Liber Pontificalis*, pp. 376, 381.

[3] See prayers in the Coptic and Armenian Liturgies, Brightman, pp. 180, 185, 438, 448. Among the Syrian Jacobites, the sacrifice is offered to the Son, pp. 87 f., *cf.* pp. 99, 102 : *cf.* Freeman *Principles of Divine Service* (Parker, 1872), vol. ii. Introd. pp. 181, 182.

Father, or in part to the Holy Trinity, in the mediation of the Son and in commemoration of His passion; and then a response of the Father, who, as it were, restores to the worshipping church their symbolic gifts of bread and wine raised to a higher power by the agency of the divine Spirit, and made to be and to convey the life-giving body and blood of the heavenly Christ for the spiritual nourishment of the faithful. In the liturgies, then, we have the highest expression of Christian worship — the worship of the thrice-holy, Father, Son, and Spirit, one God, and the worship of the Father, through the Son, by the Spirit. And we find in them constant and emphatic commemoration of the Son as incarnate, because it is as man that He has redeemed us by His sacrifice and become our mediator to give us access to the heavenly courts, and because it is as man— through His flesh and blood — that He is become the bread of life. But there is no separate worship of the incarnate Christ as specially made present on the altar in virtue of consecration. The idea of Jesus coming to

THE OBJECTIVE PRESENCE. 103

be amongst us on His altar throne and of our coming to meet Him (otherwise than in receiving Him) is conspicuously absent. The mind of the ancient church in general is represented in the canon of the African Council, " When we stand at the altar, let the prayer always be directed to the Father."[1]

If we seek to supplement the liturgies from the writings of the great fathers of the fourth and fifth centuries, we find remarkably little to our purpose. St. Chrysostom continually speaks in glowing words of the eucharistic presence and gift, but very rarely does he bid us adore or pray to Christ present to the eye of faith upon the altar.[2] Only once St. Ambrose and St. Augustine, each in interpreting the phrase in the 99th Psalm, " Fall down before (adorate) His footstool," speak of worshipping Christ or the flesh of Christ

---

[1] Hippo, A.D. 393; *cf.* Hefele, Eng. trans. iii. p. 398. To make the words of the canon exact we should add "or to the Holy Trinity."

[2] *In I. Cor. Hom.* xxiv. 5, xli. 4 (*P. G.* lxi. 204, 361). The latter passage speaks of " beseeching the Lamb who lies there (in the mysteries), who took the sin of the world " on behalf of our departed friends.

in the sacrament.[1] Besides, Cyril of Jerusalem and Theodoret each once allude to the sacramental body and blood as to be "worshipped."[2] These passages do indeed prove a belief existing which might have been developed; but their rarity, considering the whole bulk of the literature, proves that it had not been developed in fact.

How is this phenomenon to be accounted for—that in the ancient church the consecration of the bread and wine to be the body and blood of Christ, inseparable from Christ Himself, was not thought of as a special occasion for adoring Christ thus really made present?

In part probably because Christ was believed to be already present, and that too (in some sense) in His manhood, as high-priest. Where two or three should be gathered together in His name, He had promised to be in the

[1] Ambrose *de S. S.* iii. 79: "The flesh of Christ which to this day we worship (adoramus) in the mysteries." Aug. *Enarr. in Ps. xcviii.* 9: "No one eateth that flesh unless he hath first worshipped."

[2] Cyril *Cat.* xxiii. 22 (τρόπῳ προσκυνήσεως καὶ σεβάσματος); Theod. *Dial.* ii., *P. G.* lxxxiii. 168 (προσκυνεῖται).

midst of them. This was specially true in the breaking of the bread—the memorial service of His own appointment. Thus, whatever was done in the eucharist in His name, He was believed to be present and the doer of it. He was there to speak the words and consecrate the gifts. This belief in Christ already present as unseen minister anticipated and so weakened the emotion following upon the consecration. What that brought about was not the presence of Christ —He was already there—but His adoption of the church's gifts to become His body and His blood. Henceforth an attention and a worship already given to Christ as present among the worshippers was more or less focussed upon these holy symbols and instruments. But if the ancients associated His "coming" with any moment in the service, it was with the first solemn entrance of the elements, and the whole order and ritual of the service fell in with this conception.

Now Catholics with one consent still believe that Christ is in some special sense present in the whole eucharistic service, as the invisible celebrant and consecrating priest; and the more this belief is realized the less can His coming and presence be represented to the imagination as merely the result of consecration. The difference is not one of doctrine, but of practical emphasis on different parts of truth.

But also the absence of the worship of Jesus in the sacrament can only be rightly appreciated when it is viewed as part of a larger fact: *viz.*, that what Dr. Hort has called "Jesus-worship"[1] as a whole—the distinctive feature alike of Protestant evangelicalism and Catholic sacramentalism— is not at all prominent in the theology of the first five or six centuries. The phrase "Jesus-worship" must not be misunderstood. Christ in the ancient church was believed in as God, the Son of the Father, the revealer of the Father, the divine redeemer, the new life of humanity—He was believed in and worshipped, very God and very man, the second person of the Holy Trinity. But

[1] *Life and Letters of F. J. A. Hort* (Macmillan), vol. ii. p. 50.

the separate and distinctive worship of Jesus in His manhood, with all the specially tender associations of His human name—the worship which gives its special sentiment to so much mediæval and modern devotion—was but very little developed. Origen may be said to have given an impulse to it in his commentary on the Canticles,[1] and of course it existed in germ and principle from the first.[2] But it received apparently very little expansion even in popular devotion.

We cannot moreover conceal from ourselves that this type of devotion, whether among Catholics or among Protestants, whether in mission hymn-singing or in sacramental worship, has belonged to the emotional and devotional part of our manhood, rather than to the moral or rational.[3]

[1] Bigg *Christian Platonists* (Oxford, 1886), p. 188.

[2] Liddon *Divinity of Our Lord*, pp. 406 ff.

[3] *Cf.* Bishop of Rochester *The Holding of the Truth* (Rivington, 1900), p. 10: "Devotion to His (Christ's) person may be familiar and sentimental unless we feel through Him the touch and presence of the awful, infinite, all-holy God."

"Is it too much to assert that the graver danger has more than once been perilously near at hand, that the

It has belonged to that element in the religious nature which has most strangely showed its power not only to reinforce the moral will, but also to divorce itself from it. This divorce of devotion from morality has been a familiar feature both of mediæval and modern life. Perhaps the severe moral and ethical tone of the earlier Christianity—the tone which the danger of persecution enabled the church at first to maintain—held it in check. And with the severer ethical tone there went concurrently a severer theology, which lasted on after the restraints of persecution were gone. The danger of divorcing the human from the divine aspect of Christ was prevented by concentrating worship upon

---

Father has, in appearance at any rate, been obscured behind the Son, as the Son in turn behind the Virgin and the Saints?" Bigg *l.c.*

"The tender devotion of Francis [of Assisi] to the Lord's manhood became the occasion of grievous error. Everything that is compassionate in the character of the Lord was separated from His sovereign righteousness, and then these attributes of tender love were transferred to His mother, who seemed to be more within the reach of rude and simple minds." Westcott *Social Aspects of Christianity* (Macmillan, 1877), p. 111.

God, the Holy Trinity, and upon the Father through the Son by the Holy Ghost, rather than on Christ alone, much rather than on Christ as represented in His human name or His human blood.

But we are not here really concerned to estimate the legitimacy of a change in the colour of devotion. The point is only that we must treat the worship of the early church as a whole. We cannot reasonably separate the worship of Jesus in the sacrament from our whole attitude towards Him. If the early church had been in the constant habit of singing such hymns as "Jesus, Lover of my soul," is it not very likely it would have also sung, "Jesus, I adore Thee on Thy altar throne"?

For it is not possible to argue that they did not think of adoring Jesus in the sacrament because, though they spoke of the bread and wine as the body and blood of Christ, yet they did not believe this to be the body and blood of the risen and glorified Christ, very God and very man; or because they tended to conceive of the body and blood as separate from the whole person. The evidence (with the exceptions already spoken of) is strongly the other way. Certainly Cyril of Jerusalem, Athanasius, Gregory of Nyssa, Cyril of Alexandria, Chrysostom, Hilary, Ambrose, Augustine, Leo, believed that what was present in the eucharist, in some not easily definable relation to the bread and wine, was the body and blood of the glorified Christ, indiscerptible from His whole self. "Christ is in that sacrament, for it is the body of Christ."[1]

[1] Ambrose *de mysteriis* ix. 58. On the ancient treatment of the consecrated elements, outside the service of communion, see p. 299.

§ 3. *Transubstantiation considered.*

The words of our Lord, "This is my body: this is my blood," interpreted in the light of the general mind of ancient Christendom, must be taken to mean that the elements in the eucharist become by the operation of the Holy Ghost something mysterious and holy that they were not before, but without ceasing to be in all material respects exactly what they already were. The words of Irenæus express this most simply: "The bread which is of the earth receiving the invocation of God is no longer common bread, but eucharist made up of two things, an earthly and a heavenly." This very simple statement about the eucharist is introduced by Irenæus as an element in his general argument against the Gnostics, or false spiritualists of his time—that is to say, as one point among many to prove that there is no contradiction between the spiritual and the material: that as they are from the same divine Creator and Lord, so they are compatible the one with the other. The spiritual does not interfere with or overthrow the natural. " This opinion," he truly says, " is consonant with the eucharist, and the eucharist again confirms our opinion."[1]

Irenæus thus instinctively emphasizes the permanent reality of the natural elements, as he would emphasize the reality of Christ's natural manhood; though in each case, in one manner or another, the natural thing is used as an instrument or vehicle of what is supernatural, spiritual and divine, and in view of this higher use to which it is put may be said to be changed. This principle, in all its applications, represents the best and deepest and most truly philosophical mind of Christendom. This it was that guided the church aright in the fifth century, when the belief in Christ's manhood was really imperilled by a false supernaturalism or "irreligious solicitude for God." And at the period of this struggle the truth of

[1] *C. haer.* iv. 18, 5.

TRANSUBSTANTIATION.

the incarnation again consciously finds its analogy in the Christian belief about the eucharist: for there, too, the natural substance is not overthrown, though it has become something which it was not before. So Theodoret argued: "The bread and wine do not depart from their proper nature; for they remain in their former substance and shape and form." So the author of the *de sacramentis*: "They are what they were, and they are changed into something else."[1] Nothing can be plainer than these expressions of the fathers and many others.

But the monophysite tendency—that is, the tendency to absorb and annihilate the human in the divine, the natural in the supernatural—which Christian instinct, or divine inspiration in the church, checked in regard to Christ's person, so that the security of dogmatic formula was added to keep out

---

[1] See quotations in *Dissertations*, pp. 230, 274 ff. As I have argued the whole matter there at length and quoted authorities, I am only presenting it here in summary. See also Pusey *op. cit.* note G., pp. 75 ff., and note Q. pp. 162 ff. (on words implying change in the elements used by the fathers).

the invading heresy, was unfortunately suffered to prevail in the secondary region of the sacramental presence. We cannot help perceiving how easily this might have been prevented if into one of the dogmatic letters or decrees of the fifth century the familiar analogy between Christ's person and the eucharist had been introduced. But in fact the check was not provided, and the strong monophysite tendency in the theology of the Greeks went on its way in the direction of what later was called transubstantiation.

It may be said to make its first appearance in the somewhat materialistic theory of Gregory of Nyssa, that the bread and wine are, by a process analogous to that by which Christ's *mortal* body was sustained, *i.e.*, by a process analogous to digestion, converted into the substance of His glorified body in order that we may partake of it for the nourishment within us of a physical principle of immortality. But the first evidence of its having gained a clear position is to be found in by far the most influential of the later Greek-writing theologians—John of Damascus (c. 750). For, in spite of the indisputable habit of the ancients,[1] he will not allow the elements after consecration to be called types or symbols of the body and blood.[2] Such they were in their natural selves before consecration. After consecration they have become the things they typified in such sense that they have no longer the reality necessary for a symbol. For a symbol is a real thing witnessing to something beyond itself.

But while this one-sided intellectual process was going on in the East, St. Augustine was dominant in the West, and maintaining as he did a profoundly spiritual and in the truest sense sacramental doctrine of the eucharist, he long held the false or one-sided tendency in check. Not till about the ninth century did the flood from the East begin to prevail

[1] See quotations in Pusey, pp. 94 ff. and above, p. 89.

[2] *Dissert.* p. 231; *cf.* a very interesting 14th cent. Greek writer, Nicolas Cabasilas, *Liturg. Exposit.* c. 27, *P. G.* cl. 425. In the decrees of Trent (sess. xxii. c. 1), however, "under the symbol" is used as equivalent to "under the species."

in the West, and not till the eleventh century, in the famous controversy aroused by Berengar, did it successfully overcome the older tradition. Berengar, there can be no doubt, believed in a real and objective, but spiritual presence. But he contended also for the permanence of the natural elements, and that on principle. "The bread and wine are, as all scriptures attest, by consecration turned into Christ's flesh and blood, and it is certain that whatever is consecrated or blessed by God is not absorbed or taken away thereby or destroyed, but remains and necessarily becomes something better than it was."[1]

But such language was no longer tolerable. For at that period the monophysite tendency from the East coalesced with an almost brutally superstitious disposition in a very dark age of the West. Thus transubstantiation[2] in its first form,

[1] *Dissert.* p. 256.

[2] St. Peter Damian (c. 1072) appears to have been the first to use the term, *P. L.* cxlv. 883. For the formula (without the term) subscribed by Berengar, see *Dissert.* p. 257.

as for example the weak and unhappy Berengar was forced by the dominant power in the church to subscribe to it, was indeed a gross and horrible doctrine:—

"I assent to the holy Roman and apostolic see, and with mouth and heart I profess to hold as to the sacrament of the Lord's table the faith which the Lord and venerable Pope Nicolas and this holy synod, with evangelical and apostolical authority, has given me to be held and has confirmed to me: namely, that the bread and wine which are placed upon the altar are after consecration not only a sacrament but the true body and blood of our Lord Jesus Christ, and sensibly (*sensualiter*), not only in a sacrament but in reality, are handled by the hands of priests and broken and bruised by the teeth of the faithful."

Most of the contemporary writers against Berengar assert that the body and blood of Christ are to be eaten and drunken "with the mouth of the body as well as the mouth of the heart"; and, like some of the earlier Greeks, they deny that the elements after consecration retain their natural properties of nourishing or becoming corrupted or being digested. The nature of the bread and wine was understood to be destroyed in everything but appearance. Miracles were recklessly postulated, and it was sufficient objection to any more reasonable treatment of the mystery that in diminishing the difficulty of belief it reduced the merit of faith. Certainly the atmosphere in which the doctrine of transubstantiation grows into a dogma is calculated to send a shiver through one's intellectual and moral being.[1]

But the rising scholasticism, or perhaps the evidence of facts,[2] very quickly corrected this extreme tendency. The use indeed of the distinction of substance and accidents, for the purpose of assisting the doctrine of transubstantiation, was already familiar

---

[1] *Dissert.* p. 258.

[2] Painful mischances to the consecrated hosts appear to have been very common—" negligentia ministrorum evenire solet," says Abelard: see *Dissert.* p. 260.

to Berengar, and he excellently combats the proposed use of it, denying that accidents can exist apart from their substance (or "subject"), or apart from that of which they are attributes. But the later scholastics used the distinction with a more laborious precision to formulate the doctrine. By the act of consecration the substrata or substances of the bread and the wine were changed into the substances of the body and blood of Christ: but the accidents or qualities of bread and wine—all that we are cognizant of in our experience of bread and wine—remained with all their natural properties and defects; remained (in the compassion of God) as veils under which the awful realities should be screened.[1] In later days a still further refinement has led Roman theologians to say that the remaining species or accidents of the bread and wine constitute a real object—"something

[1] Not, however, as accidents of the new substances of the body and the blood, but as accidents inhering in no substance. This is declared to be *de fide*, and Roman writers, modern as well as mediæval, exult in the numerous violations of the natural order involved in transubstantiation.

objectively real." But this is in fact to explain away the doctrine and the phrase. Plainly modern philosophy of all schools recognizes no distinction between substance and accident—knows no substance other than that "something objectively real" which is constituted by the qualities or relations under which alone any object is known in experience. Thus the modern Roman theologians allow to the consecrated bread and wine all the reality which any one believes any bread and wine to possess, or, in other words, explain away transubstantiation, till it remains as little more than a verbal incumbrance due to an inopportune intrusion into church doctrine of a temporary phase of metaphysics. In its original and more natural meaning, transubstantiation—the overthrowing of the natural substance by the spiritual—is truly contrary to a fundamental Christian philosophy, and really "overthroweth the nature of a sacrament."

But even in its minimized sense transubstantiation does not remain only as an incumbrance in terminology, witnessing to a mistake in the dogmatic action of the mediæval church: for its really materialistic and unspiritualizing effects cannot be done away. As soon as the accidents or species have reached a certain stage in the process of being digested by the communicant, or of being destroyed in some other way, it is felt to be irreverent to imagine that they can still be veils of the divine substances. Thus a reversal of the process of transubstantiation is postulated, by which the supernatural substances are withdrawn, and the natural substances (of bread and wine in process of digestion or corruption) are restored, and the accidents have again "a subject to inhere in."[1]

But the result of so materialistic a way of conceiving the relation of the spiritual gift to the outward part of the sacrament is that the corruption of the material elements involves the withdrawal of the divine gift. Thus the coming of Christ to the Christian through Holy Communion is in Roman

[1] See *Dissert.* p. 270, 271, and J. R. Milne *Doctrine and Practice of the Holy Euch.* (Longmans, 1895), p. 67.

theology and books of devotion spoken of as a temporary visit which, though certain fruits may remain, is yet in its primary sense, as an indwelling of Christ, over when the digestion of the material food begins— it is suggested after a quarter of an hour. " This day," so devotion is taught to express itself, " my Lord

> " Came to my lowly tenement
>   And stayed *awhile* with me."

Or

> "Oh, when wilt Thou *always*
>   Make our souls Thy home?
>   We must wait for heaven,
>   Then the day shall come."

Now such an idea of a temporary visit of Christ to the soul is in most marked contradiction to the teaching of the undivided church. " He is held for a moment in your hands, but He is wholly resolved into your heart," says Chrysostom. " What you see " in the sacrament, says Augustine, " passes away, but the invisible thing signified does not pass away but remains."[1] The whole

[1] Chrys. *Hom. in Ephes.* iii. 4 (*P. G.* lxii. 281): Aug. *Serm.* 227. Similar language is used by later Western

teaching of the fathers on the subject seems indeed to be a loving commentary upon our Lord's words about His *abiding* in us and we in Him.

Enough has probably been said. Apart from the degree of authority which transubstantiation has obtained in the West, and to a certain extent in the East, there is truly on the grounds of antiquity, or Scripture, or reason, nothing to be said for it. And we cannot admit the weight of an authority which fails in these supports.[1]

theologians: *e.g.* Raymund of Sabunde *Theol. Nat.* tit. 285 (in the 15th cent.) speaks of Christ as the spiritual food of the eucharist converting the Christian gradually and permanently into Himself. This implies an abiding union. But the doctrine stated above is, I believe, now accepted in the Roman church.

[1] See also below, p. 220.

§ 4. *The gift and presence spiritual.*

It is the general assertion of the church that the presence of Christ, or of His body and blood, in the eucharist is spiritual—"not bodily but ghostly," as our English Archbishop Aelfric so earnestly contended.[1] And I may assume at this stage that the word spiritual as applied to the eucharistic presence means something more than presence "*to our spirits.*"[2] It describes a certain condition of the thing given, in itself; though its relation to our spirits belongs, as will appear, to its very essence. What then is it that is to be understood in this connection by the word "spiritual"?

Of course it expresses not what is unreal, but what is profoundly real. The things that are not seen, of which the whole of

---

[1] For his position and teaching, see Hunt *Hist. of the Engl. Church to* 1066 (Macmillan, 1899), pp. 375 f.

[2] So Jeremy Taylor, see below, p. 235.

visible nature is in a manner the symbol and the sacrament, are for the Christian the supremely real and actual and present things. In whatever sense then we approach and receive the body and blood of Christ in the eucharist as spiritually present, it is certain that they are in the deepest sense real and really present.

Beyond this it is easy enough to say that by calling them spiritually present we mean that they are present in such a way as is to be quite dissociated from any idea of the movement of material particles—a spiritual presence is a non-material presence. And this may well be perfectly true—though the more the modern physicist investigates the ultimate nature of matter, the more he breaks down all the supposed barriers between matter and spirit; but it is not in any case the most important truth. It is possible to maintain a profoundly unspiritual view of the presence of Christ, and still to erect a supposed safeguard by asserting that He is present under the form of bread and wine, in His body indeed, but after the manner of spirit and without any interference with material law, and not locally or materially as in heaven. Certainly if the spirituality of Christ's presence means this, it means also something more positive and more moral: something more on the lines of the scriptural use of the word spiritual.

Any thing or process then, whether material or no, is, according to the New Testament use of the word, spiritual in which the Holy Spirit, or generally spiritual purpose, effectively manifests itself, and which it effectively controls. Isaac was born "after the Spirit" by contrast to Ishmael, who was born "after the flesh,"[1] not because he was less materially born, but because the divine Spirit was specially evident in the circumstances of his birth. Thus even Christ's mortal body we should call in one sense spiritual, because it acted according to a controlling spirit of holiness, and all He did in the body He did spiritually. It was "in eternal spirit" that He offered Himself without spot to God. But, on the other hand, the

[1] Gal. iv. 29.

grossness of our earthly nature, the likeness of the flesh of sin, still—except so far as He was miraculously exempted from its restrictions — more or less limited Him. "All authority" was not yet "given Him in heaven or in earth." "The Spirit was not yet given, because Jesus was not yet glorified." He had a baptism to be baptized with, and how was He "straitened till it was accomplished!"[1]

Thus the risen body of Christ was spiritual in a very different sense; not because it was less than before material, but because in it matter was wholly and finally subjugated to spirit, and not to the exigencies of physical life. Matter no longer restricted Him or hindered. It had become the pure and transparent vehicle of spiritual purpose. He rose from the dead (as is apparently implied in the narrative of St. Matthew),[2] leaving the gravestone undisturbed. The angel rolled it away to show that He was risen. He

[1] Matt. xxviii. 18; John vii. 39; Luke xii. 50.
[2] "He is not here," the angel says, "for he *rose*" ($\dot{\eta}\gamma\acute{\epsilon}\rho\theta\eta$). Matt. xxviii. 6. This the fathers insist upon: Pusey *l.c.* p. 56.

appeared immediately, and apparently in familiar form, to the faithful women, and later in the day "in another form" to the two disciples on the way to Emmaus—unrecognizable by their yet carnal eyes. His outward appearance, as St. Gregory remarks, was relative to their inner mind;[1] and subsequently, when "their eyes were opened, He vanished out of their sight." Immediately after, He is present in Jerusalem among the apostles without any opening of their closed doors, but yet to exhibit to them the attributes even of the mortal body, by eating with them as of old. Henceforth, during the forty days, He never lived with them in the life of earth, but was manifested from time to time as His spiritual purpose required.

Now, from the physical point of view, such spiritualization of matter as is involved in this conception of a spiritual body, is becoming perhaps—I will not say more imaginable, but more and more conceivable: less out of

---

[1] "Hoc egit foris Dominus in oculis corporis quod apud ipsos agebatur intus in oculis cordis." *Hom. in Evang.* xxiii. 1. *P. L.* lxxvi. 1182.

analogy with our ultimate conceptions of matter. But the important point to notice is that the spirituality of the risen body of Christ lies not so much in any physical qualities as in the fact that His material presence is absolutely controlled by His spiritual will. The disciples, for example, could no longer argue with any approach to security that He was where they had last seen Him, until they had evidence that He had left that spot. All such subservience to conditions of space was over for ever. His manifestations were manifestations to special persons—*i.e.*, those whose faith He willed to rekindle—under special forms for special purposes.

And if all *subjection* to conditions of space was over for the body of the resurrection, even more certainly was it over for the glorified body (if any distinction is to be drawn), the body in which He through His whole person has become "quickening spirit," and even His flesh and blood are "spirit and life." As to what the "body of glory" is, silence is our best wisdom. We feel sure indeed that He retains "all things appertaining to the perfection of man's nature"; and with St. John we believe that He not only has come, but also is to come again in the flesh.[1] But it is not in the flesh and blood of our present conceptions, which "cannot inherit the kingdom of God"; nor have we any faculties to conceive the glory of which even our material nature in Him is susceptible. It is enough for us to know that in the perfection of our nature, but in glory inconceivable, He still exists; and it is out of this glory that He feeds us with the flesh and blood which are spirit and life.

Once more then what do we mean by the spirituality of this gift or presence of Christ in the eucharist?

It is commonly asserted both by Romans[2] and Anglicans that His presence in the eucharist is different in manner from His presence in heaven: that He is not present in the eucharist materially, nor after the

---

[1] 1 John iv. 2—3, 2 John 7. "Cometh" means "is to come again." See Westcott *in loc.*

[2] See app. note 9, p. 296.

manner of a body, nor strictly locally—though no doubt the Anglican would be clearer and more unimpeded in these denials than the Roman. As was remarked above, our notions of what materiality fundamentally means are becoming increasingly vague. But at any rate the presence is "after a spiritual and heavenly manner," of which we can learn nothing by scientific analysis.

But it is of much more importance that in claiming spirituality for Christ's presence we claim for it that, though He condescends to use material means, the sacramental elements, yet He is never subject to them. As in the risen and glorified body in itself, so in its sacramental application to our necessities, spiritual purpose dominates everything with an absolute freedom. The presence is controlled by the purpose. And in a matter where the evidence of the senses is denied us, our only right to be confident that the presence abides with us, depends on our remaining under the shelter of the purpose.

Thus it seems to me to be illegitimate and insecure to argue that because the presence, admitted to be spiritual, is vouchsafed to us (so to speak) under conditions of bread and wine, therefore I am justified in assuming that it abides under those conditions so long as the bread subsists, or till I am informed to the contrary. For such an argument is wholly based on the limiting and restricting conditions of material existence—on conditions of existence to which Christ was subjected in His mortal body, but not in His resurrection body; and still less (if the two are distinguishable) in His body of glory. If the disciples could not with any degree of security argue after His resurrection that He must still be in Jerusalem or in Galilee, or in such and such a spot, for He was seen there and they had no reason to believe that He had stirred—much less is it open to us to argue that His presence under conditions of bread and wine abides till we have reason to believe it is removed. The bread and wine are instruments of His will which He can at pleasure use or discard; and to which He is in no subtlest way subjected. The only secure argument is that the gift was given for a certain purpose, and so long as that purpose is observed we have absolute reason to trust that His promise will not fail us. So long as that which controls our actions is His "name," and that means in part His will and purpose, so long, and so long only, can we be sure that He is "in the midst of us."[1] And if this condition applies to His presence in all assemblies of the church for worship, it applies specially to His special presence in the holy eucharist.

It may be worth while in this connection remarking that we have no right to carry out the analogy of the incarnation and the eucharist so far as to say that the union of the supernatural and the natural elements is an indissoluble union in the latter case as in the former. It is not indissoluble, just as also it is not personal, or "hypostatical" as the technical phrase goes. There is in fact an analogy in fundamental principle between the incarnation and the sacraments, but it does not admit of being carried out in detail.

A *spiritual* presence in the eucharist then,

[1] Matt. xviii. 20.

whatever else it may mean, means this: like the appearances after the resurrection, it is a presence to certain persons for certain purposes. What then, we proceed to ask, is the purpose of the gift and presence?

It is plain that the purpose for which the divine gift in Holy Communion is given is indicated by the symbolism of bread and wine—it is that we may (in Goethe's words) partake of a heavenly under the form of an earthly nourishment. The sacrament was instituted in order to be eaten. It was not "by Christ's ordinance," or in accordance with any expressed intention of His, "reserved" (except so far as the reserving is necessary for the communion of sick or absent brethren),[1] "lifted up, or worshipped"—constituted, that is to say, an external object or centre of worship here on earth. And, indeed,

---

[1] Of reservation for the purposes of communion, such as the ancient church practised, I do not think it can with any fairness be denied that it falls inside the scope of Christ's revealed intention; though no doubt also it falls within the competence of any part of the church to decide how the sick or absent are to be communicated: see app. note 10, p. 298.

the intention with which the bread and wine are consecrated to become for the church the body and blood of Christ is constantly expressed in the liturgies. With one consent the church in her prayers of consecration has prayed that the elements of bread and wine may by the power of God be made or declared to be Christ's body and blood *for a certain purpose*, viz., "in order that those receiving them may be confirmed to holiness; may obtain remission of sins and . . . eternal life," [1] "for the remission of sins and eternal life to them that receive," [2] "that as many of us as by participation from the altar shall have received the holy body and blood of Thy Son, may be fulfilled with all heavenly benediction and grace," [3] "that it may be a legitimate eucharist for all those who receive it." [4] The same restricted intention is constantly and almost without exception illustrated in the language of the fathers. They

[1] Clementine, Brightman *l.c.* p. 21; so the Lit. of St. James, p. 54; of St. Mark, p. 135, *cf.* p. 180, etc.

[2] Syrian Jacobites, p. 89.

[3] Roman canon.

[4] Gallican: Neale and Forbes *op. cit.* p. 4.

but expressed Christ's words: "Take, eat; this is my body: drink ye all of it; for this is my blood."

Thus admittedly the gift of the body and blood are given to the Church under the forms of bread and wine, in order to be received. What we are to " do in remembrance of Him " includes, as its chief feature, the taking and eating the bread and wine which are declared to be His body and blood. Even the sacrificial efficacy of the eucharist depends, as will appear, upon reception; and the adoration of Christ's body and blood in the sacrament occasionally spoken of by the fathers is so spoken of mostly as a preparation for the act of communion—" no one receives without first adoring."[1]

This being the clearly-expressed original and catholic idea of the sacrament, we cannot fail to be struck with the apparently light-hearted security with which this obvious intention of the sacrament according to the mind of Christ has been enlarged in later practice. Communion of the people in

[1] See p. 104.

western Christendom came to be an occasional and exceptional feature in the celebration of the eucharist, or an additional service. The sacrifice and the worship were largely divorced from the communion. But more than this: the wholly legitimate reservation of the consecrated elements, that the absent sick folk might be communicated from the one altar and the one loaf, became—what was quite unknown to the ancients, and remains alien to the customs of the orthodox East—a reservation of the sacramental body in order that, inasmuch as with His body Christ is present in His whole person, the church might have a permanent external presence of Christ in the midst of her in a particular spot in the church. Thus the sons of faith might go to be near Him and adore Him, for His "delight is with the sons of men"; and His loving condescension has made Him the "prisoner of the tabernacle," and leads Him to give Himself to be "exposed" for worship, and in the service of Benediction to bless His people with a blessing like that of His uplifted hand, behind the veil, so to speak, of the enshrining wafer.

No doubt the theologians of the Roman church have had an uneasy conscience about these developments. They have not been developments of theological science, properly so-called; they have been developments of popular devotion which, because they could not be restrained, theological authority has more or less reluctantly sanctioned. Yet in effect the sanction has been given. This devotion to the sacrament in the modern Roman church is, I do not say the most real, but the most conspicuous form of Christian devotion, or has no rival except that to the mother of our Lord. Yet it is a most serious lowering of the level of Christian devotion if a permanent external presence of Christ amongst Christians comes to be the most usually entertained idea of the manner of His "abiding with us," instead of the only sort of abiding which the New Testament suggests—the indwelling of Christ *in* the members of His body, of which it is the glory of the sacrament to be the earthly instrument. This institution of an external shrine of the divine presence among Christians, with its subtle but profound influence on Christian thought and language and devotion, is, I repeat, a tremendously bold development in view of Christ's institution. It ought to raise in all minds a deep questioning of the authority of the Church to innovate so freely upon His intention: but also it cannot but raise in many minds the question whether, where the purpose of the sacramental presence is so vitally changed, we have the right to feel secure of the permanence of the presence itself.

Does not the conception of a spiritual presence, with its absolute independence of its material vehicles, with its unshackled liberty from moment to moment to be or not to be at the will of Him whose presence it is, lead us to believe that fidelity to the declared purpose for which it is given is the sole security for its permanence ? Does not any other standard of security really reduce the presence to material conditions —to conditions, that is, of attachment to physical nature such as belonged to Christ only in His mortal body?

I know it is said by some practical persons, Is it not a pity to argue the question? What real difference does it make whether there be in fact any presence in the tabernacle other than exists anywhere else? Is not God everywhere present? Is it not true of the whole Christian life that we "are come unto Mount Zion, and to the heavenly Jerusalem . . . and to Jesus, the mediator of the new covenant, and to the blood of sprinkling"? What if the truth be that the little flickering lamp and the tabernacle do but enable the worshipper to realize what, after all, in the tabernacle and out of it, is, apart from theological refinement, substantially true? To which the answer seems to be: it may matter very little in the case of this or that individual at this or that moment. But the devotion as a whole has a general tendency, and the general tendency is hardly that of enabling one to realize the universal presence of God in the world, or the constant presence of all Christians, at all times and in all places, to the heavenly things, or the indwelling of Christ in the soul of the individual and in the living church. The indisputable tendency of this devotion, and of the theology which reduces even the gift of communion to a temporary visit, is towards a conceiving of Christ's presence with the church as local and external—a conceiving of it which becomes more and more remote from St. Paul's or St. John's or St. Augustine's.

And if uses of the sacrament other than those strictly covered by the divine intention are, in a high degree, alluring and comforting and popular, we must remember that the easiest sort of Christian devotion is not always the truest. Christian worship may be, nay must be, meant to involve spiritual effort. It is God's intention that we should be spiritually lifted up to realize that Christ's presence with us now is a presence in the church, as the life of the body, not amongst Christians as in an outward shrine; and that nearness to Him, or remoteness from Him, is a matter of faith and holiness, and not of place.

The eucharistic presence then, because it is

spiritual, is a presence for a certain divinely-defined purpose; and (as a consequence of this) it is a presence to certain persons—that is, the sons and daughters of faith. So the risen Christ appeared only to those who had faith, or in whom it could be reawakened, and He appeared, according to His will, differently to different people.

In other words—the eucharistic presence, because it is spiritual, is relative to the faith of the church, and presupposes "holy persons" to receive "holy gifts."

This appears in the prayers of the liturgy. Thus in the Roman mass the prayer runs "that this oblation may become *to us* (*nobis*) the body and blood of Thy dearly beloved Son": and in Greek liturgies there is a prayer for the consecration of the communicants as well as the gifts, "that the Holy Spirit may come upon us and upon these gifts": and the solemn cry just referred to, which invites to communion, is "the holy things for the holy persons."[1]

---

[1] *Cf.* Brightman *op. cit.* pp. 59, 135, 329, and St. Cyril's comment on τὰ ἅγια τοῖς ἁγίοις, *Cat.* xxiii. 19.

This follows indeed from considerations already entertained; for the gifts are given to be eaten, and while the outward elements are received by the lips and eaten like other food, it is plain that no physical organs can appropriate the accompanying spiritual gift. Plainly "the means whereby it is received" must be faith. Thus Mozley when, in the passage already quoted,[1] he has emphatically asserted that the fathers held "the objectiveness, as we now call it, of the inward part or thing signified in the sacrament," yet continues: "We see at the same time, upon examination of their language, that this objectiveness was held with a very important modification, which gives a double aspect to the doctrine of the fathers. The modification was this, that the body and blood of Christ could not be eaten except by faith, which was the medium by which this spiritual food had any operation or function as food. Although, therefore, the body and blood itself followed an external test of presence, as being the concomitants of the

[1] See above, pp. 72—3.

material elements, the eating of this body and blood followed an internal test, and was the concomitant entirely of the state of mind of the recipient." . . . "To suppose that a man's natural mouth and teeth can eat a spiritual thing would be a simple confusion of ideas." This is the point of Augustine's celebrated phrase "*Believe* and thou hast eaten."[1]

There is, indeed, in patristic language on this subject a certain ambiguity, as in the original language of Scripture. In St. John vi. the eating Christ's flesh and drinking Christ's blood is plainly regarded as possible only for those who thereby "have eternal life"—who "abide in Christ and Christ in them": the wicked and such as are void of a lively faith plainly are excluded from *this* eating. On the other hand, our Lord said, "This is my body," simply, and St. Paul talks of the evil-disposed "not discerning the [Lord's] body"—not appreciating, that is to say, what at the

[1] *In Jo.* xxv. 12: Quid paras dentes et ventrem? Crede et manducasti.

THE PRESENCE SPIRITUAL.

same time he received like the others.[1] This ambiguity continues in the fathers—some saying that the same gift is received to profit or to condemnation, or with varying degrees of profit according to the proportion of faith; others using language such as definitely implies that without faith there is no reception of the spiritual realities. Thus Origen writes about "the Word who became flesh and the true food, which whoso eateth shall certainly live for ever, no bad man being able to eat it. For if it were possible for a man while he remains bad to eat the Word who was made flesh and the living bread, it would not have been written that 'he that eateth this bread shall live for ever.'"[2] And Cyprian records a miracle—how a defaulter from Christ attempted to eat the holy body of the Lord and found a cinder in his opened hand; and this he takes for "proof by a single instance that the Lord with-

[1] There is a similar ambiguity in the N. T. language about baptism: for St. John always speaks of "him who is begotten of God," *i.e.*, the regenerate, as if he must be living accordingly: see 1 John iii. 9—10, v. 4, 18.

[2] *In Matt.* tom. xi. 14.

draws when He is denied, and that which is received is of no profit to salvation to those who do not deserve it, since the Holy One fleeing away,[1] the saving grace is turned to a cinder." And Jerome says: "All who are lovers of pleasure rather than lovers of God . . . do not eat the flesh of Jesus nor drink His blood."[2] And Leo the Great warns his hearers against doubting the reality of the body of Christ in the sacrament, because "it is what you believe with your faith that you receive with your mouth; and in vain that they say Amen who argue against what is received."[3] And Augustine repeatedly: "He who abides not in Christ and has not Christ abiding in him, without a doubt neither eats His flesh nor drinks His blood, but rather eats and drinks to his judgment the sacrament of so great a thing." "It is as if Christ said: He who does not abide in Me and in whom I do not abide, must not say or imagine that he eats My body or drinks My blood."[4]

[1] *De laps.* 26: sancto (*a. l.* sanctitate) fugiente.
[2] *In Isai.* lxvi. 17 (tom. iii. p. 506, Paris, 1706).
[3] *Serm.* xci. 3.
[4] *In Jo.* xxvii. 18; *de civ.* xxi. 25. *Cf. Dissert.* p. 234.

Elsewhere, however, both St. Jerome and St. Augustine express themselves as if the faith of the recipient made no difference to the thing received. "It was none the less the body of the Lord and the blood of the Lord even to those to whom the apostle said, He that eateth unworthily eateth and drinketh judgment to himself."[1] There is, in fact, an ambiguity in their language like the ambiguity of the Scriptures on which they comment. The gift on the one hand is what it is by divine consecration, and on the other hand it is what it is for faith; and it requires faith not only to appreciate but to entertain and receive it.

This question whether the wicked receive the body or flesh of Christ in the Holy Communion long remained an open one. Paschasius Radbert in the ninth century speaks with great ambiguity.[2] Rupert of Deutz (c. 1130) uses almost contradictory

---

[1] Aug. *de bapt. c. Donat.* v. 9. *Cf.* Jerom. *adv. Jovin.* ii. tom. iv. pars ii. p. 218.

[2] *De corp. et sang.* vi. 2.

phrases.[1] At some subsequent date—later than the twelfth century—the solution arrived at was that the wicked receive the "res sacramenti" (the body and blood), but not the "virtus" or beneficial effects. The English church in the 29th Article returns to the earlier and more ambiguous language of Augustine.

In fact, if we hold on the one hand with the ancient church the objectiveness of the gift, and on the other hand not only that men can derive no benefit from sacraments except so far as they receive them well, but also that the eating of Christ's flesh and blood is (in St. John vi.) a spiritual act of which only those who have a living faith are capable, the remaining differences can only really be verbal. We cannot really define what occurs when a personal gift of God

---

[1] See *P. L.* clxix. 470, where he says: "The bread once consecrated never afterwards loses the virtue of its consecration, or ceases to be the body of Christ; but it does not profit an unworthy person." But see also clxx. 40, where he says: "Into him who has no faith nothing of the sacrifice can enter except the visible species of bread and wine."

which is meant for faith, is presented to some one totally without faith or the desire of it—totally without fellowship in the faith of the Church. The question is only one stage removed from the question of what would occur if the sacrament were eaten by an animal without reason—to which the Master of the Sentences replies, " God knows."[1]

And it is of real importance that we should recognize that faith—the common faith of the church—probably plays the same part in actually constituting the spiritual reality of the sacrament as the common reason of man does in constituting the objects of the natural world : that is to say, we should expect spiritual objectivity to

[1] Peter Lombard *Sententt. lib.* iv. dist. 13. The determinations of St. Thomas Aquinas on these points (*S. Th.* iii. qu. 80, art. 3)—in which he disowns " some of the ancients "—are plainly based upon considerations involved in transubstantiation which really *subject* Christ to material conditions. Dr. Pusey *l.c.* p. 37, says : " The belief in the real presence may indeed be maintained without it [the belief that the faithless eat the body of the Lord], if it be held that God withdraws that presence in such cases." So Cyprian seems to have held, and Ephrem Syrus and others are quoted in the same sense.

follow the same law of relation as natural objectivity.

No doubt to hold that the faith of the church goes to constitute the spiritual reality of the presence, so that for one who is altogether outside that faith the spiritual reality cannot be said to exist—to hold this, some men would say, is equivalent to denying its objective character. But they would say this in their haste; because it had not fallen in their way to study metaphysics, which is the science of first principles of reality as known to us.

Metaphysical study makes us conscious how much the mind (the perceptive or intellectual faculties in us as distinct from the moral or spiritual) has to do with actually constituting the objects of the outward world—the trees, the animals, the persons. Mind, as it is in me and in all men, not only perceives these things as ready-made, but also has to do with making them to be. God, we commonly say, creates things in nature, and He creates mind. But in fact the two creations are inseparable. The

things have no existence apart from the minds which know them, for it is only as held together by the mind of the observer that all the sensations of colour, taste, hardness, softness, shape, etc., coalesce into an object held together in relations to the whole orderly world. Relations are the work of mind, and relations are necessary to make objects. On the other hand, it is only the sensations given from outside which enable the mind to perceive and know, and so to become a mind at all. This is a perplexing and irritating conclusion perhaps, but it is apparently inevitable if one likes to think. And it would be of a piece with this if we are to suppose that a similar relation exists between the spiritual presence of Christ in the eucharist and our corresponding faculties of spiritual perception:—
if we are to suppose that, though it is God who makes the bread to be the body of Christ and not man (as it is God who makes the objects in the natural world and not man), yet He makes this spiritual reality to exist relatively, not absolutely: in such

sense as to exist only for faith, the faith of the believing and worshipping Church, just as He creates the world relatively, not absolutely, that is, to exist for rational beings and by the action of thought.

And we observe that this doctrine of relativity makes the reality of objects, neither in the sphere of nature nor of the spiritual world, to depend upon the precarious state of mind of any individual. The trees and flowers do not depend on *my* mind for their existence, but on the action of that common reason in which all men more or less effectively share, but which, at the bottom, has its origin out of the divine reason. Upon mind in general, however, the existence of the world as we know it does depend; and for irrational creatures—such as in no way share in reason—it cannot in any real sense be said to exist; for existence on analysis proves to mean a relation to mind. So the spiritual presence of Christ in His body and His blood (and all that goes with it) rests not on the precarious faith of any individual, but is so relative to the faith of the church as a whole—that common faculty which rests at bottom on the activity of the Holy Ghost—as that apart from faith, or for one who in no way shares it, it can no more in any intelligible sense be said to exist than the beauty of nature can be said to exist for what is quite without reason. For here again existence proves to mean a relation to a consciousness —only now it is not mere rational sensibility, but spiritual faith.[1]

A few words in conclusion may be said to those who will feel a lack of definiteness in the account of the real presence just given. You have asserted, they will say, an objective presence but at the same time have pleaded against phrases being exclusively or freely used which suggest a localized presence. You insist that the presence is not physically

[1] It is interesting to reflect how any right doctrine of the spirituality or relativity of the divine presence enables us to recognize that there can be *degrees* of divine presence, such as are postulated in St. Matt. v. 34-5 and in many other places. Degrees of divine presence are possible in proportion as it expresses divine purpose and is relative to human faith.

attached to the elements, but is secure only in proportion as we abide under the shelter of the purpose for which it is given. You claim that it is a presence for faith in such sense that it may be said only to exist in relation to faith. But by making these and the like qualifications you are taking away the sharp outline of the Catholic belief and leaving it hazy and dim. To which the reply, I think, is threefold.

First, some such qualifications are found in almost all careful theological statements on this subject—such as the statement already quoted from Cardinal Newman. Surely it takes the edge off the later western way of regarding the sacrament, if Christ does not descend from heaven upon our altars, and does not move when the host is carried? And if this is the accurate truth, it needs surely to make its influence felt on the popular faith—perhaps, as the fathers seem to have felt, by the simultaneous use of different kinds of metaphors for the presence, more or less neutralizing one another.

Secondly, and more generally, there is a kind of clearness of statement which suits material objects but which simply does not apply to spiritual things, and it is plain that such clearness is, both in the Bible and the fathers, avoided as a danger. Nothing is in fact more striking than the constant anxiety of the fathers to make men feel that human language can but dimly adumbrate, and not fully or precisely define, divine mysteries. They continually appear to shrink from being too clear-cut in their explanations. In our days we seem greatly to need the reminder of Hooker (applicable to other parts of the revealed truth besides the incarnation) that "because this divine mystery is more true than plain, divers having framed the same to their own conceits or fancies are found in their expositions thereof more plain than true."

Thirdly, I should like to suggest that it is a shallow rationalism and intellectual indolence, rather than the simple faith of the poor (or poor in spirit), which crave for clearness of statement beyond the measure allowed to us who " see through a glass, darkly "; and the craving must be gratified only with great reserves. We have admirable examples of ancient teaching—about the sacraments, among other things. Who ever taught a town congregation of average intelligence better than St. Chrysostom, or simple people better than St. Augustine? And they use great plainness of speech without materializing truth or brushing aside the atmosphere of mystery which blunts the too sharp edge of doctrinal statement.

CHAPTER III.

THE EUCHARIST A SACRIFICE.

§ 1. *The church's sacrifices.*

THERE can be no question that from the earliest days the Christian church thought of the eucharist as a sacrifice.[1] This is implied by Clement of Rome when he sees in the eucharistic worship of the church, and the "offering of the gifts," a continuation under new conditions of the ordered sacrificial worship of the old covenant.[2] And the word is plainly used of the eucharist (however inadequately conceived) in the *Didache*: "On the day of the Lord come together and break bread and make your eucharist, after having first confessed your transgressions that your sacrifice may be pure."[3] And Justin Martyr speaks

---

[1] Harnack *Dogmeng.* Bd. i. 152, n.[1].
[2] Clem. Rom. *ad Cor.* 40—44.   [3] *Did.* xiv. 1.

repeatedly of "the sacrifices through His name, which Jesus the Christ delivered to us to make—that is at the thank-offering (eucharist) of the bread and of the cup"; and of "the bread of the eucharist which for a memorial of His passion Christ our Lord delivered to us to offer."[1] Finally, to go down no farther than the second century, Irenæus is emphatic that it is not that sacrifices are abolished under the new covenant, but only that their character is changed; for Christ "took the bread which is of this (lower) creation and gave thanks, saying, 'This is my body': and likewise the cup . . . and confessed it to be His blood, and taught the new oblation of the new covenant which the church receiving from the apostles offers to God over the whole world."[2] There was no doubt about it. The eucharist was a sacrifice. It was the eucharist which the prophet foretold when he said, from God,

[1] Justin *dial. c. Tryph.* 41, 117. The word "eucharist" passed from meaning simply thanksgiving to mean the specially ordained thank-offering of the Christians as above; and then the consecrated elements: see above, p. 6.

[2] Iren. *C. haer.* iv. 17, 5.

"In every place . . . shall be offered unto my name . . . a pure offering."[1] And the eucharist was specially called the "spiritual" (or "rational") and "bloodless" sacrifice: spiritual—a worship "in spirit and in truth" none the less because it was a visible and corporate act, offered in connection with visible symbols; and bloodless—in the first sense, no doubt because the symbols were bread and wine and not the flesh and blood of animals, but also because these clean and less gross elements had been associated already with spiritual conceptions of worship.[2]

The fathers used this sacrificial language, we must remember, while at the same time the Greek and Roman world was looking upon them as eccentric for holding a religion

---

[1] *Didache* xiv. 3; Justin, Irenæus, Clement, Tertullian, etc.

[2] "Bloodless" is used by Philo, of the meal offerings (*de anim. sacrific.* ed. Mangey, ii. 250), but also of inward as opposed to outward worship (*de ebreit.* i. 370; *cf.* ii. 254). Similarly it is used in the *Test. of xii. Patr.* (*Levi*, 3) of the worship of the angels, "a rational odour of sweet savour and a bloodless offering." There is an obvious ambiguity which remains in the earliest Christian use of the word.

without altars and temples, as well as without images.[1] And indeed they are constantly proclaiming that (in the sense of the heathen) they had none of these. For they interpreted *their* sacrifices to mean, as in fact in their origin they did, that God had physical appetites and needed animal or material sustenance. "They sacrifice fat victims to God as if He were hungry, and pour out wine as if He were thirsty."[2] But the Christians knew that God does not stand in need of any material offering—of blood or sweet savours. He made all things and needs none of them.[3] "We offer Him (what alone He asks) a bloodless sacrifice and the rational service." "We approach Him only with pure prayer." The purified heart and the acceptable prayer are the only sacrifices He asks for, and sanctified hearts and bodies the only temples in which He will dwell.[4] This is

[1] Origen *c. Cels.* viii. 17; Minucius Felix *Octav.* 10.

[2] Lactantius, *Divin. Instit.* vi. 2.

[3] Justin M. *Apol.* i. 13; Athenagoras *Legatio*, 13; Tertullian *Scap.* 2.

[4] Clem. Alex. *Strom.* vii. 3, 14; Greg. Naz. *Orat.* ii. 94—95.

THE CHURCH'S SACRIFICES.

the constantly reiterated Christian protest against heathendom.

And it must be borne in mind that the fathers of the first four centuries mostly took a low view of the sacrificial system of the Jews, which they regarded as not directly ordered by God, seeing it had its origin from " Gentile grossness," but as something which God at the best tolerated among them to avoid worse things, or even laid on them for a punishment;[1] so that on this side also they are anxious to separate themselves from fellowship with a sacrificial system as commonly understood.

But all this language of disparagement of material sacrifices still leaves them on their own ground recognizing that the worship in spirit and in truth is not a mere inward and individual approach to God, but a corporate and therefore outward thing—a worship which publicly acknowledges God in all His

[1] See *Lux Mundi* (small ed.), p. 241, n.¹; and Freeman, *Principles*, vol. ii. p. 56. In spite of Augustine's influence, the view appears still in Rupert of Deutz *Dial. int. Christ. et Jud.* ii. (*P. L.* clxx. 581-2) : "Deus legem illam non jussit sed admisit; non voluit sed permisit."

gifts, though He needs them not;[1] and a worship which finds its central expression in the eucharist, in which, according to the ordinance of Christ, bread and wine are presented to the Father, in the name of the Son, and in memorial of His passion, with the adoration and prayer and thanksgiving of sons, and blessed by the Holy Spirit to become the Lord's body and blood, and partaken of by the worshippers that they may be bound all together in Him. That was for the Christians the chief and central expression of rational service and bloodless sacrifice.

Now we must examine somewhat more closely what the eucharistic sacrifice does and does not mean, on the background of the New Testament teaching, but postponing for the moment the question of the witness of the New Testament to the eucharist in particular.

Whatever may have been the original and

---

[1] Iren. *C. haer.* iv. 18, 6 : " For we offer to Him, not as if He needed ought, but giving thanks to His supremacy and sanctifying the creature."

fundamental meaning of sacrifice, it had come among the Jews to mean especially something given to God in homage and recognition, or to recover His favour. The prophetic teaching, which especially influenced the early Christian church, had already purged this practice of offering material gifts from the notion that God in any sense needed material things for Himself. "I will take no bullock out of thy house, nor he-goats out of thy folds. For every beast of the forest is mine. . . . The world is mine, and the fulness thereof. Will I eat the flesh of bulls, or drink the blood of goats? Offer unto God the sacrifice of thanksgiving." Thus it had become plain to any thoughtful Jew of the later period that, if God required sacrifices, that was because of what they represented — the obedient will and spirit; the private, and still more the corporate, acknowledgment of God as the source of all blessings; the desire to hold communion with Him; above all the desire to recover His favour where it had been lost by sin. For this idea of propitiation had come to predominate among all the possible conceptions of sacrifice.

But here was a chief point of contrast between Jew and Christian. For when the Jewish passed into the Christian church, it became a first principle that there was no more need for propitiating God. God, without any co-operation from the race He was redeeming, had provided His own propitiation. He had sent His own Son, in our flesh, and "given Him up" to be the voluntary victim of human sin, and thereby also the expiation for it. By His willing offering of Himself as Son of Man, in a perfect obedience through life and unto the shedding of His blood, He had made reparation in man's name for man's sin. He had done, spiritually and effectually, once and for all, what the one inaugural sacrifice of the old covenant and the annually recurring day of atonement had done symbolically, but outwardly only and ineffectually: He had set the redeemed humanity, the church of the redeemed—His own body—on a new basis with God. They, as associated with

Himself, had in Him been once for all effectually reconciled to the Father; and so long as they retained their hold on Christ by faith, and the obedience which springs of faith, they were accepted "in the beloved."

For the Christian, therefore, there was no more need of any propitiation. Christ, their effective propitiation, was triumphant and alive at the right hand of the Father in all-powerful intercession. It remained for them only and in all ways to make thankful commemoration of His victorious passion and resurrection, by their whole bearing "to proclaim the Lord's death till He should come again," and to intercede and plead in fellowship with His intercession — in His name and in the power of "the blood of sprinkling," the "blood of the eternal covenant."

But the abolition of any further need for *propitiation* was not equivalent to the abolition of *sacrifice*. Those sacrifices of the old covenant to which in the Epistle to the Hebrews Christ's sacrifice is chiefly compared, are, we should notice, the inaugural sacrifice at which Moses spoke the words "This is the blood of the covenant which the Lord hath made with you,"[1] and the sacrifice of the great day of atonement. And these were not simply two among many sacrifices; they held a position of their own. The one inaugurated a whole covenant of worship, and the other (in the fully developed ritual system) maintained it in being by annually purging first the priesthood, and secondly the holy place, the altar and the whole tabernacle, from the uncleanness of the people.[2] Thus the purpose of the ritual of the day of atonement was to purge and renew the whole sphere of sacrifice, and enable the various offerings of the year following to be made without offence.

All this, according to the teaching of the Epistle to the Hebrews, was an ineffective shadow, but a real shadow of what was to come. Christ Jesus, our great high priest and victim, self-sacrificed upon the cross

---

[1] Exod. xxiv. 8: *cf.* Hebr. ix. 15—24; Matt. xxvi. 28.
[2] Levit. xvi. 11, 16, 18, 20.

and self-presented in the heavenly place, has for those who belong to Him by faith made all things new. He has "taken away" their sin. He has inaugurated for them an everlasting covenant of worship. He has opened heaven. He has given them "freedom of approach." That is to say, He has made possible—in perpetual reliance on His merits and His Spirit—the life of sacrifice as it belongs to accepted sons and not to trembling slaves.

We must remember that it is specially appropriate for our present purpose to quote the Epistle to the Hebrews, because in this epistle, alone among the books of the New Testament, the atonement wrought by Christ is approached from the side of ritual and worship;[1] because there alone is the explanation of the sense in which the *worship* of the old covenant was to be fulfilled and not destroyed under the new: there is the climax of all that teaching about the holy and priestly people consecrated to the worship

[1] See Dr. A. B. Davidson's admirable commentary (Clarks), pp. 196 ff.

of Jehovah, of which the ritual law as a whole, especially "the law of holiness,"[1] and the prophecy of Ezekiel and many of the Psalms are the gradually deepening expression. And I may add (by anticipation) that the Epistle to the Hebrews has special points of affinity with the language of our Lord's institution of the "breaking of the bread."

Thus the abolition of any further need for propitiation is not the abolition of sacrifice. It is but the setting free of humanity to offer, unimpeded by the alienation which sin had caused, the sacrifices proper to man—not because he is a trembling sinner, but because he is a forgiven and accepted son, and knows what he owes to God for his creation and his redemption.

The New Testament then is full of the idea of the church as a priestly body, or (what is the same thing) of the church as offering sacrifices. It is "the continual sacrifice of praise, the fruit of lips which make confession to God's name"; or it is

[1] See Exod. xix. 6 and Lev. xvii.—xxvi.; also Ezekiel (with commentary by A. B. Davidson, *Cam. Bible for Schools*).

the sacrifices of almsgiving and of doing good "with which God is well pleased";[1] or it is the sacrifice of ourselves, that is, our bodies offered by ourselves "as a living sacrifice, holy and acceptable to God, which is our reasonable service";[2] or it is the sacrifice of prayers and intercessions;[3] or the sacrifice of sufferings borne on behalf of the whole church in fulfilment of Christ's sufferings;[4] or, finally, it is the sacrifice of other men won and consecrated and offered to God individually and collectively.[5] And the first Christian theologians were full of this thought. Christ, according to Clement of Rome and Origen of Alexandria, is "the high priest of our oblations."[6] He has entered into the holy place for us once for all, says Origen again, and our day of atonement lasts till the end of the world; but we must supply Him with the spiritual counterpart of the "sweet incense beaten

---

[1] Hebr. xiii. 15—16.   [2] Rom. xii. 1.
[3] Rev. v. 8: *cf.* 1 Tim. ii. 1, 1 Pet. ii. 5.
[4] Col. i. 24 in the light of Phil. ii. 17.
[5] Rom. xv. 16 ; Col. i. 28.
[6] Clem. Rom. *ad Cor.* 36; Origen *de Orat.* 10.

small" wherewith the high priest of the old covenant filled his hands. As He stands before God, He looks to see with what sort of offering every church and every individual is filling His hands.[1]

Irenæus, again, comparing the new covenant with the old, declares that "it is not that sacrifices as a whole have been abolished, but only that the kind of sacrifices has been changed." And the characteristic of the Christian kind of sacrifices he finds in this, that they are the "sacrifices of sons," acceptable not in themselves but for their sakes who offer them. "Sacrifices do not sanctify a man; but his conscience who offers, being pure, sanctifies the sacrifice and makes God accept it as from a friend."[2] Thus if we

[1] *In Levit. Hom.* ix. 5, 8: "considerat quid offeratur." He is spiritualizing the meaning of Leviticus xvi. 12.

[2] Iren. *C. haer.* iv. 18, 2—3. This may sound strange, but it is the ultimate Christian principle; and of course what makes it possible is that behind the Christian offerers, and embracing them in Himself, is the one priest in whom alone is any offering acceptable. *Cf.* the prayer of the Leonine Sacramentary: "Mercifully, O Lord, look upon the offerings *(hostias)* of Thy people, and that they may become acceptable to Thee, let the salutary coming of Thy Holy Spirit cleanse our consciences." *P. L.* lv. 41.

want a general heading under which to bring the sacrifices of the new covenant, we should say that they are *spiritual* sacrifices, *i.e.*, sacrifices in which the enlightened and redeemed will or spirit is at work; sacrifices, therefore, which are always of persons, and of things or rites only as adjuncts and expressions of persons. And to this principle we shall find ourselves brought back later on.

But because these redeemed persons are not isolated individuals, but an organized body, this sacrificial life of theirs must find a corporate expression, and such expression the eucharist is. The eucharist may be viewed therefore, first of all, as an occasion (such as, without any divine institution, the church might have devised for herself) for representing corporately her sacrificial character—a service in which the church as a body comes before the Father, conscious of her sonship, and offers the sacrifice of praise and thanksgiving, commemorating God's mercies in creation and redemption; and the sacrifice of prayer in the name of Christ and the power of His propitiation; and the sacrifices of alms for the poor and fruits of the earth and products of her skill, to symbolize that "all things come of God, and of His own do we give Him"; and, finally, offers herself as a glad instrument of the purpose and kingdom of God.[1] And all this the eucharist was. Irenæus makes a great deal of one aspect of the eucharist —the offering of the fruits of the earth— which might have belonged to a Christian service without any special institution of Christ or any special eucharistic gift or presence.[2] And early canons suggest that a Christian eucharist in the first age must have frequently resembled a modern harvest thanksgiving.[3]

[1] It ought to be remarked that the assumption ot eucharistic worship always was that the worshippers were "in a state of grace." Where this standing-ground had been lost the church ordinance designed for its recovery was penitence or penance, followed by readmission to communion.

[2] See app. note 11, p. 300.

[3] See *Canones Hippolyti* iii. (29), xxxvi. (186 ff.); *Can. Apost.* 3; *Const. Apost.* viii. 39 f. At Rome till the ninth century the people, and the clergy too, continued to bring their offerings of bread and wine; and, in a certain form,

But of course these associations of sacrifice only gathered round the eucharist because Christ had, at His last paschal supper, taken the bread and cup of wine, and blessed them, and said, "Take, eat: this is my body; drink this: this is my blood"; and ".This do in remembrance of me." Here we have a "continual remembrance of the sacrifice of the death of Christ" ordained by Christ Himself, both in word and act. And it is plain that what from the first gave special efficacy and meaning to the prayers and worship of the Christian eucharist was this central fact: that is to say, the fact that Christ instituted in the "breaking of the bread" a special memorial of His sacrifice; and, secondly, announced the bread and wine of this memorial to be His body and His blood, to be eaten and drunken by His disciples.

What bearing, then, has this ordained consecration and communion upon the eucharist considered as a sacrifice?

the custom survives at Milan and in parts of France: Duchesne *l.c.* p. 165.

§ 2. *No repetition of the sacrifice upon the cross.*

First, we will set aside an effect which consecration does not have. It does not effect any renewal of the sacrifice of the cross—any renewed surrender of Christ to death. Symbolically, no doubt, in the breaking of the bread and the outpouring of the wine, and in the separate consecration of the bread and of the wine,[1] there is represented the violation of Christ's body and the outpouring of His blood, and the separation of the blood "which is the life" from the body in death; and this symbolical representation is accompanied by the sacred words of Christ which point its meaning; and the whole of this sacramental action is directed Godwards, to the accompaniment of a prayer, and not manwards as

[1] Thomas Aq. *S. Th.* p. iv. qu. lxxvi. 2, lxxviii. 3. This idea, however, is not apparently ancient.

a (so to speak) dramatic or instructive action. We have thus a solemn commemoration before God of the sacrificial death of Christ. But the death, or the humiliation which belongs to the death, is commemorated only, not renewed or repeated. When the fathers speak of an "immolation"—*i.e.* a fresh sacrificing of Christ in the eucharist—they are referring only to the symbolism of the sacrament, not to its inward reality; and this, in the language of the church taken as a whole, is quite unmistakable, and continues to be so as late as the theology of St. Thomas Aquinas. A few quotations will make this plain.[1]

"The flesh and blood of this sacrifice," says Augustine, "before Christ's coming was promised in victims that were types: in the passion of Christ it was rendered up in very reality: since Christ's ascension it is celebrated in the sacrament of memorial."[2] "We offer," says Chrysostom, "but as making for ourselves a memorial of His

[1] See also app. note 12, p. 302, on some ambiguous language.   [2] Aug. *c. Faust.* xx. 21.

death ... We make always the same sacrifice; or rather we effect a memorial of the sacrifice."[1] "That which is offered and consecrated by the priest," says Peter Lombard, "is called a sacrifice and oblation because it is a memorial and representation of the true sacrifice and of the holy immolation made once for all upon the cross: and Christ once died upon the cross and was there immolated in Himself: but He is daily immolated in the sacrament, because in the sacrament is a remembrance of what was once done."[2] "It is called a sacrifice," says St. Thomas, "with reference to what is past: inasmuch as it is commemorative of the Lord's passion which was the true sacrifice." "It is a representative image of Christ's passion, as the altar represents the cross on which He was once immolated."[3]

The eucharist then is not in the stricter

[1] Chrys. *ad Hebr. Hom.* xvii. 3.
[2] Petrus Lom. *Sentt.* iv. 12, 7.
[3] Tho. Aq. *S. Th.* Pars iv. qu. lxxiii. art. 4, qu. lxxxiii. art. 1. The schoolmen, it may be mentioned, paid immense attention to the doctrine of transubstantiation, but very little to that of the eucharistic sacrifice.

sense of the term propitiatory. It is certainly in accordance with the language of the New Testament to reserve this term for the initial act by which Christ gave humanity a new standing before God and opened the kingdom of heaven to all believers.

It is, however, impossible to deny that the word propitiatory in a wider sense may be applied, and from the days of Origen has been applied, to the eucharist. Thus Jeremy Taylor says: " As all the effects of grace and the titles of glory were purchased for us on the cross and the actual mysteries of redemption perfected on earth, but are applied to us and made effectual to single persons and communities of men by Christ's intercession in heaven; so also are they promoted by acts of duty and religion here on earth, that we may be 'workers together with God,' as St. Paul expresses it, and in virtue of the eternal and all-sufficient sacrifice may offer up our prayers and our duty; and by representing that sacrifice may send up, together with our prayers, an instrument of their graciousness and acceptation. . . . It follows that the celebration of this sacrifice (the eucharist) be in its proportion an instrument of applying the proper sacrifice to all the purposes which it first designed. It is ministerially, and by application, an instrument propitiatory; it is eucharistical, it is an homage and an act of adoration; it is impetratory, etc."[1]

The use of the word propitiatory of the eucharist, or the refusal to use it, may thus be said to be a mere matter of language. But there are deep reasons of religion, as well as scriptural authority, to move us to restrict its application; and of course still deeper reasons for guarding the truth, which the restriction expresses, of the uniqueness and all-sufficiency of the sacrifice of Calvary.

Only comparatively late in the history of theology does this truth, that the sacrifice once made was "full, perfect, and sufficient," seem to have been imperilled. First, at the end of the middle ages, when the idea was

[1] *Life of Christ*, pt. iii. § 15.

widely current that the sacrifice of the altar was a distinct addition to the sacrifice of the cross; for while the sacrifice of the cross had been offered once for original sin, the sacrifice of the altar was daily offered for actual sins. This doctrine is unhesitatingly asserted in sermons ascribed in one form to Albertus Magnus, and in another to St. Thomas Aquinas, but really representing a later and lower opinion; and its currency is attested by the way in which the early Reformers speak of it, and by the repudiation of it in the Confession of Augsburg, and in our Thirty-first Article.[1]

And again, in the later and deliberate theology of the Roman church, a view has come to prevail—I believe that is not too strong a term—of which it is exceedingly difficult to bear the statement: a view which involves in each mass in some real sense a re-sacrificing of Christ.

To constitute a sacrifice it is supposed —quite contrary to ancient opinion—that there is required some *destruction* of the

[1] See app. note 13, p. 304.

object sacrificed in honour of God.[1] Thus if the mass is a proper sacrifice, and if the subject offered in sacrifice is Christ, it follows that in each mass Christ must surrender Himself to a certain sort of destruction—in other words, that though the victim in the sacrifice of the altar is identical with the victim of the cross, yet the act of being sacrificed is distinct. In the mass we have always the same perfect victim, but in each mass a re-sacrificing of Him. And, further, it appears that the essence of this renewed sacrifice lies in this: that Christ in the mass submits at the priest's hands to become food for man under the form of bread. And this submission to a condition of becoming food, a condition unnatural to the human body, is on each occasion a fresh self-emptying—a fresh con-

---

[1] "Communiter docent doctores intervenire debere destructionem aliquam rei oblatæ." Einig (see below, p. 306), p. 108, who gives quotations. It is in part this narrowing of the idea of sacrifice which has brought with it in later Roman theology the almost exclusive attachment of the mass to the moment of Calvary rather than to Christ's perpetual presentation of Himself in heaven.

NO REPETITION OF CHRIST'S SACRIFICE.

descension to an inferior state, and thus a fresh sacrificing of Christ.[1]

Such views as these—whether popular misconceptions or theological errors—which involve in each eucharist some addition to the sacrifice of Calvary or some real renewal of it, there can be very little need to combat in this country to-day. But it has been necessary to mention them in order to show that in maintaining with care and anxiety that the sacrifice by which we were redeemed upon the cross was one, full, perfect and sufficient, so that it can need no supplementing and admits of no renewal, we are not now, and our forefathers in the sixteenth century were not, fighting a phantom.

And there is a third view, exceedingly difficult to understand, for which a number of Anglicans have undoubtedly made themselves responsible, and which is evidently still current among us, according to which there is postulated in the eucharist some real presence of the flesh and blood of Christ

[1] See quotations in app. note 14, p. 305.

as they were when He was dying or dead upon the cross.

The true view, as I cannot but call it, is expressed in a phrase of Rupert of Deutz: "It is the whole Christ who is present, the whole Christ who lies upon the altar: not that He may again suffer, but that to faith, to which all past things are present, His passion may be represented by way of a memory."[1] That is to say, it is the "whole" or living Christ, Christ as He is, that is made present to us, and given to us in the eucharist; but it is a certain momentous event in the past, an event of eternal significance which to faith is ever a present reality, which is there specially commemorated—His death upon the cross. It is the living Christ who feeds us with His own life: but it is as alive out of death: it is "the Lamb as it had been slain."

Now it is natural enough that those who adopt a merely commemorative view of the eucharist should say that it is the dead Christ Who is presented to us there, in the sense that a past event in history is presented

[1] See *de Trin. et opp. in Gen. lib.* vi. (*P. L.* clxvii. 431).

to our contemplation. But it seems wholly unintelligible how divines who in any sense believe in a real presence can speak of the eucharistic body—one hesitates even to write the words—as " the corpse " of Christ, or use language which is certainly highly misleading, unless they mean—which God forbid—that there is in every eucharist a body sacrificed afresh and blood shed anew in death.[1]

Now we may dismiss these painful mistakes. For there is welcome at all hands, in the Roman Church as well as outside it, for the truth of the sufficiency of the once made atonement. The sacrifice of the Son of Man once offered in death has been accepted in glory. In the power of that sacrifice Christ ever lives, our high priest and perpetual intercessor, the continually

[1] Andrewes, *Sermons of the Resurrection*, vii. (vol. ii. p. 301 f.): "Christ's body that now is. True; but not Christ's body as now it is, but as then it was, when it was offered, rent and slain. . . . By the incomprehensible power of His eternal Spirit, not He alone, but He as at the very act of His offering is made present to us . . . we must repair even *ad cadaver.*" *Cf.* Freeman *l.c.* ii. Introd. pp. 152, 153; see also *Report of Round Table Conference* (Longmans, 1900), pp. 44 f., 49 f.

accepted propitiation for our sins unto the end of time. All that we need to do or can do is to make thankful commemoration, in His way and by His Spirit, of His redemptive sufferings, and to unite ourselves to His perpetual intercession, where He presents Himself for us in the heavenly places, or as He makes Himself present among us in our eucharistic worship. "Ye are come unto Jesus the mediator," and to "the blood of sprinkling"—that is, of perpetual application. Meanwhile, if the church has been offering many sacrifices at many altars, whatever value they have or have had must be because the church which offers is a priestly body by union with Christ's unique high priesthood, and what she offers obtains its ratification through union with His sacrifice.

§ 3. *The connection between the earthly and the heavenly offering.*

Having thus got rid of a great misapprehension, we must now return to the question —In what way does the consecration of the elements to be the body and blood of Christ, and the communion in these holy and effectual symbols, affect the sacrificial action in the eucharist?

There was in ancient days no single and precise answer to the question. But we can trace three, not incompatible, attempts to express the truth.

(1) The consecration of the earthly offerings to become, for the church's food, Christ's body and blood, in accordance with the institution of Christ, was understood to mean that they had been accepted, with all the accompanying prayers, at the heavenly altar, and united to Christ's heavenly offering.

This conception may be made plain by a little explanation. It has been already noticed that the form of consecration most commonly in use in the ancient church was a prayer for the descent of the divine Spirit, or the outpouring of the divine power, to consecrate the elements upon the earthly altar. But in the Roman canon the place of this prayer is apparently taken by another which expresses the idea that the earthly elements are to be conveyed by the hands of the holy angel to the heavenly altar in the sight of the divine majesty, and so united to the divine realities within the veil that they shall be returned for the Church's participation as Christ's body and His blood.

This idea was in Irenæus' mind when he asserts the existence of the heavenly altar as necessarily presupposed in eucharistic worship, and says "Thither our prayers and offerings are directed."[1] It is the same thought which is expressed in many of the liturgies where they dwell upon the " glorious

[1] Iren. *C. haer.* iv. 18, 6: "There is therefore an altar in heaven; for it is thither," etc.

interchange" or "commerce" between earth and heaven, and pray that God having received the oblations of the church upon His heavenly altar for the savour of a spiritual sweet smell, like the sacrifices of the fathers of old, would send down in return the gift of divine grace, or give us in their place for corruptible things incorruptible, for earthly heavenly, for temporal eternal.[1] For whether the effect of consecration is expressed as the descent of a heavenly presence to earth, or as the lifting up of earthly gifts and hearts to heaven—and both expressions were understood to be only attempts to render with the imperfect instrument of human language what was not really any process in space at all[2]—in either case the reality to be expressed involved the mingling of earthly and heavenly

[1] See the prayers in Brightman *l.c.* pp. 23, 59, 129, 390, and the western *secreta* at the offertory *P. L.* lv. 29, 148; also app. note 15, p. 306.

[2] Ambrose *de S. S.* i. 11: "He appears to descend when we receive Him to dwell in us. . . . To us He appears to descend, not that really He descends, but that our minds ascend to Him." Ambrose, however, is not specially referring to the eucharist.

things; the acceptance of earthly gifts and, as the evidence of their acceptance, the fulfilling of them with a heavenly power.

It is this view—that the human prayers and sacrifices are, by eucharistic oblation and consecration, accepted at the heavenly altar and returned to the church as the spiritual food of Christ's body and blood — which appears to underlie the original structure of the liturgies. For all the intercessions appear originally to have stood more or less exactly where they stand in the Gallican rites,[1] and in our own Communion Service, at the beginning of the service. And after the oblation of the earthly elements to God and the invocation of the Holy Ghost upon them, all mention of sacrifice and all intercession was over—except, indeed, in the saying of the Lord's Prayer. The giving back of the gifts as Christ's body and blood

---

[1] For the Gallican rite see Duchesne, pp. 189, 199. The same position for the intercessions is implied in the Ethiopic *anaphora* where they are presupposed (Brightman, p. 189). In St. Mark's liturgy and the Nestorian they appear within the *anaphora*, but at the beginning only and before the invocation.

THE OFFERING IN HEAVEN. 189

was the evidence that the sacrifice was accepted and united to the eternal sacrifice.

Of this view of the acceptance of the sacrifice, a late and interesting expression may be quoted from Paschasius Radbert,[1] somewhat at length. The man who is living apart from God and yet comes to the altar "thinks," Paschasius says, "only of what he sees, and does not understand that the flesh of Christ is really received from nowhere except from His hand, and from the heavenly altar at which He, as 'the high priest of good things to come,' stands on behalf of all. Therefore the priest, when he begins to offer *(immolare)* these gifts, says among other words: 'Command that these things may be carried by the hand of Thy holy angel to Thy heavenly altar, etc.' And dost thou imagine, O man, that thou canst receive that thing from anywhere else than the altar on high where it is taken to be consecrated?"

Then explanation is made of the local

[1] Paschasius *de corp. et sang.* viii. 1, 2 (*P. L.* cxx. 1286 f.).

terms "carrying up," etc. It is of the very essence of a mystery or sacrament that something should be transacted beyond what is seen. This invisible transaction is outside conditions of space. "God is a Spirit, and is illocally present everywhere. So you must understand that these spiritual gifts are neither locally nor carnally carried on high before the presence of the divine majesty." Their lifting on high is their being consecrated. "Do you imagine that the altar at which Christ stands as high priest is anything else than His body, through which and in which He offers to the Father the prayers of the faithful and the faith of the believers? And if the body of Christ is truly believed to be the heavenly altar, you will perceive that from nowhere else than Christ's body can you receive His flesh and blood."

Again he insists that, because Christ is the real consecrator, the value of the consecration is independent of the merits or demerits of the earthly priest. " For before it [the oblation] becomes by consecration the body of Christ, it is the oblation of the priest, as he professes, or of the whole Christian family which offers it: but by the word and truth of the Holy Spirit it becomes a 'new creature' in the body of our Creator for our restoration's sake. Therefore He is shown by the evidence of Scripture always to stand by the heavenly altar; that from His offering of Himself *(immolatio)* we may receive His body and His blood. But the priest, because he seems in outward appearance to take the part of Christ between God and His people, sends up the gifts of the people by the hand of the angel to God and receives them back again, made effectual by the body and the blood, and distributes them to one and all, not as being what the outward vision suggests, but what faith apprehends."

This then was a view of the sacrifice which maintained itself for a long time. We present our gifts and sacrifices, and in doing this we have done all that we can. We offer them for acceptance on the heavenly altar in the name of Christ, and they come back to us as His body and His blood, fulfilled with all the fruits of His passion. And this means that all our prayers and offerings have been united to the abiding sacrifice and offered by the Heavenly Priest.

(2) But a second view followed in the wake of the first at no long interval, differing perhaps rather in words than in reality, —a view which associates itself naturally with the Greek, or as we may say the normal, as against the unusual Roman, manner of consecration. The Holy Ghost is, according to the normal rite, invoked to consecrate the elements lying upon the earthly altar. And in virtue of this consecration they become for the church the body and blood of Christ; that is to say, the " Lamb as it had been slain,"—but who is alive for evermore, our perpetual and never-failing propitiation— becomes present in the midst of the worshipping people in His body and blood of sacrifice, and they become present to Him. In a special sense they " are come unto . . . Jesus the mediator and the blood of sprinkling." Thus the consecration, of itself and

THE OFFERING IN HEAVEN.

prior to communion, effects a special nearness of the church to the one sacrifice: a nearness expressed in the well-known modern hymn:

> " And now, O Father, mindful of the love
>   That bought us once for all on Calvary's tree,
> And *having with us Him that pleads above*,
>   We here present, we here spread forth, to Thee
> That only offering perfect in Thine eyes,
> The one true, pure, immortal sacrifice."

For, granted this view of a near, but as yet external, presence of the One Sacrifice among the worshippers, it naturally followed that this should become the special occasion for the church to offer, though only in the sense of presenting or pleading, this sacrifice—the special occasion, that is to say, for the body to join with the Head in His unceasing heavenly action; and, once more, it became equally natural that the sacrificial intercessions of the church should be moved forward to this solemn point from their position at the beginning of the liturgy, or should be repeated after the consecration.

And this doctrine of the effect of consecration is found from early days. Already in Cyprian we find the teaching—though it admits of somewhat different interpretations—that Christ, as the high priest after the order of Melchizedek, in offering bread and wine at the institution of the eucharist offered also His own body and blood, or Himself, to the Father, and that what He did the priests of the church are to do, and that thus "the passion of the Lord is the sacrifice which we offer."[1] And already in the Clementine liturgy, and in the eucharistic prayers of Serapion, and in the liturgy described by St. Cyril (all about A.D. 375), the intercessions are reiterated and completed after the consecration. And St. Cyril gives the reason. It is when by the consecration "the spiritual sacrifice, the bloodless service, is perfected," that "over that sacrifice of

---

[1] See Cypr. *Epp.* lxiii. 4: "He offered bread and wine, that is His own body and blood." 14 He "offered Himself to the Father and bade this be done in commemoration of Him; so that that priest truly fulfils the functions of Christ who imitates what Christ did, and he offers in the church a true and full sacrifice to the Father in so far as he begins to offer as he sees Christ to have done" (*i.e.*, with the mixed cup). 17 "The passion of the Lord is the sacrifice which we offer."

propitiation we entreat God on behalf of the common peace of the churches, for the tranquillity of the world," and generally for the living and the dead: and he repeats, it is because "we believe that it will be the greatest benefit to the souls for whom the prayer is offered, while the holy and most awful sacrifice lies before God."[1]

It must be admitted that, in the deepest sense immediately to be considered, the "spiritual sacrifice" is not "perfected" except in communion; and it might be supposed that doctrine such as St. Cyril's would lead more easily than that previously described to the separation of the idea of sacrifice from that of communion—a separation always disastrous where it is allowed to prevail. It is interesting, therefore, to observe that St. Chrysostom, in whom this second view of the sacrifice is specially prominent, is also specially insistent against the

---

[1] Cyril *Cat.* xxiii. 8, 9. This remains the standard doctrine of the sacrifice in the East: see Nicolas Cabasilas *Liturg. Expos.* 27 (*P. G.* cl. 425); and *cf.* John Johnson *Unbloody Sacr.* (Libr. of Anglo-Cath. Theol.) i. p. 341.

separation. He loves to teach how, when the priest "invokes the Holy Spirit" upon the elements, and so " completes the sacrifice," the worshippers are with the eye of faith to " see Christ sacrificed and lying," and "the priest standing and praying over the sacrifice, and all reddened with the precious blood." They are to realize that they "have come near to the blessed and uncorrupted nature," to the " things in heaven," to the body which is at the right hand of the Father, but which is present in the power of the Spirit representing His death, who is " a Lamb as it had been slain."[1] " And how," he asks, " when the whole people stands stretching out their hands, a priestly body all complete, and the awful sacrifice lies there in view, how can we fail to gain God's favour by our intercessions " (for the departed of whom he is speaking) ? Yet, as is well known, he was most emphatic in resisting the rising practice of attending at

[1] Chrys. *de sacerdot.* vi. 4, iii. 4, 5, *de bap. Chr.* 4, *de cœm. et cruc.* 3, *in Phil. hom.* iii. 4 (*P. G.* xlvii. 681, 642—3, xlviii. 369, 398, lxii. 204).

THE OFFERING IN HEAVEN.

the eucharist without communicating. He certainly will not allow that we can take our proper share in the sacrifice except by communicating. "Art thou not worthy of the sacrifice or of the participation? Then neither art thou worthy of the prayer," *i.e.*, of assisting at the service. Those who cannot receive should go away with the penitents.[1]

In fact, if it be kept in clear view that our real fellowship in the sacrifice is only maintained by communion—of which more hereafter; and if it be remembered that the phrase about the earthly sacrifice being carried up for consecration to heaven, and that about the Holy Spirit coming down to consecrate the sacrifice on earth, are both of them figures of speech to express a mingling of earthly and heavenly things which cannot really be rendered in terms of space, the difference between the two views which we have been considering fades away and vanishes. The earlier practice expressed

[1] *In Ephes. hom.* iii. 4 (*P. G.* lxii. 29). This was not, however, the opinion of all the fathers: see app. note 16, p. 307.

in the liturgies was to present the earthly prayers and sacrifices at the heavenly altar, in view of an acceptance already guaranteed for them by the general freedom of approach which belonged to Christians, as well as by the particular eucharistic promise and institution of Christ. The later practice was to repeat these sacrificial prayers when the consecration of the elements according to Christ's institution had given the church a fresh assurance that their priest and sacrifice was in the midst of them. The difference is rather imaginative than real. In both views what gives its value to the church's sacrifice is its being offered on the heavenly altar of Christ's perpetual self-presentation. " He offers Himself as priest. . . . Here in 'image' or under a veil, there in naked truth where He presents Himself as our advocate with the Father."[1] Both alike avoid the great pitfall in eucharistic doctrine —the putting the eucharistic sacrifice in line, so to speak, not with the heavenly presentation or pleading of the sacrifice of Christ,

---

[1] Ambrose, see app. note 17, p. 308.

but with the slaying of it on Calvary. And we have a good deal of reason to be thankful that what is indisputably the true background of eucharistic doctrine—not the Lamb being slain, but the Lamb as it had been slain—is what our best and most popular eucharistic hymns present to the imagination of English churchmen.[1]

(3) It is common to both the views of the eucharistic sacrifice which have just been stated—though the second leaves perhaps more opportunity for ignoring it—to recognize that the sacrifice is consummated in communion. That this must be so in the deepest sense a little consideration will show us.

The end of Christ's offering of Himself *for* us, as our propitiation and our representative, is that humanity as a whole—all men, so far as they will allow it to be so—may finally in Him be brought back into union with God and with one another. What He

[1] We owe in this matter a debt of gratitude hardly to be exaggerated to Dr. Bright, but also, before him, to the Wesleys, whose *Eucharistic Manual* for Methodists (republished by Hodges, 1880) contains remarkable hymns on *the Eucharist as a sacrifice*, pp. 112 ff.

does first for us, He must ultimately do in us. "For their sakes I consecrate myself, that they also may be consecrated in truth."[1] And the way in which we are brought to share Christ's acceptance with God is, not merely by an external imputation of His merits, but by a real incorporation into His life by His Spirit. "Now *in* Christ Jesus ye that once were far off are made nigh in the blood of Christ: . . . reconciled," St. Paul explains, "in one body" by the working of one Spirit; "for through Him we both (Jew and Gentile) have our access in one Spirit unto the Father." "The Father hath reconciled you in the body of Christ's flesh through death, to present you holy and without blemish and unreproveable before him."[2] Thus our Lord cannot be our representative priest and sacrifice in an effective sense unless we go on to share His life. His sacrifice for us can only be "consummated in" us.[3] We must share it both actually and

---

[1] John xvii. 19. [2] Eph. ii. 13—18, Col. i. 22.

[3] This expression is actually quoted from Pseudo-Dionysius *de eccl. hier.* iii. 12 (*P. G.* iii. 444); but it represents the

morally. Actually we must become " of His body," and morally we must share in the life of His Spirit. And this participation can come about through no effort of ours. It must be purely a gift of the divine grace. And it is this gift which in fact is communicated in " the breaking of the bread." There we eat His flesh and drink His blood, and so are admitted to share in fullest measure the fruit of His sacrifice, which is nothing less than the fellowship in His life. Thus only by communion can we in any effective sense share the eucharistic sacrifice, so far as that sacrifice is not a merely human effort, but is identified with Christ's offering, and attains thereby its spiritual validity. Only in Christ can we offer and plead Christ. We have an altar whereof we are to eat.

It is because it expresses so fully this principle that the essential end of sacrifice is communion with God and in God, the sharing of the divine life—a principle which

whole theology of the fathers: see Thomassin's admirable section, *Dogm. Theol.* " De Inc. Verb. Dei," lib. x. cc. xxi. f.

had been obscured under the old covenant—that the eucharist is really the realization of all that the untaught, or half-taught, instincts of man had been feeling after in the practice of sacrifice all over the world. And that this is the principle of the eucharist is what all the best Christian theology maintains. St. Thomas Aquinas will have it that the pre-eminence of Christ's priesthood over that of the old law lies in its effects: and that its effects are communicated by participation: "wherefore in the new law the sacrifice of Christ is communicated to the faithful under the species of bread and wine."[1] Again, " He who offers the sacrifice must participate of the sacrifice "—that is, communicate.[2]

It needs to be observed that when Chrysostom and other ancient writers are speaking of persons being present at the whole eucharistic service without communicating, they do not speak of their "taking part in the sacrifice," but of their "taking part in the

[1] Tho. Aq. *S. Th.* pars iii. qu. xxii. art. 6.
[2] *L.c.* qu. lxxxii. art. 4. Unfortunately he only applies this to the *priest:* but see below, p. 213.

THE OFFERING IN HEAVEN. 203

prayers."[1] It may be much better for church-people to take part in the prayers than to be absent altogether; but we can never allow ourselves to use language which implies that those who do not communicate can really take part in the sacrifice, or that "non-communicating attendance" is the *normal* Christian act, without giving currency to a view of sacrifice which is less than Christian. That the sacrifice is completed in communion is the effective witness of all the liturgies. It is rooted in the vital principle that what in our manhood Christ is, that we are through and in Him to become. "Hear us, O God of our salvation," says an ancient eucharistic prayer, "because we trust that through these holy interchanges that is to be effected in the body of the whole church, which took place first of all in its Head."[2]

The church, in the well-known formula, is to be the extension of the incarnation. The whole Christ is to consist of the Head

---

[1] See pp. 307-8, and *cf. canon. Nicaen.* 13, *Ancyran.* 4, 5, 6.
[2] *P. L.* lv. 37—reading *commercia* for *mysteria* according to the MS.: *cf.* Feltoe's edition.

and the members sharing the same life. And from this point of view it is impossible to doubt that the fathers would have resented the sharp distinction drawn in recent theology between the "natural" body of Christ—in heaven and (according to the terminology referred to) also in the eucharist—and the mystical body, the Church. They are perpetually reiterating that we become His body by sharing His body: that by eating His flesh we pass into His flesh.[1] They do really make the spiritual principle of Christ's manhood the new life of the Church, and think of Christ as making us His body by (as it were) gradually absorbing us into Himself. "If you are the body of Christ and His members, it is the mystery (or sacrament) of yourselves that is laid upon the altar. It is the mystery of yourselves that you receive. It is to what you are, that you say Amen. For you will hear 'The body of Christ,' and you will reply Amen."[2]

Thus it is the teaching of the fathers that

---

[1] Thomassin (*l.c.* cc. xiv., xxi., xxii.) multiplies quotations.
[2] St. Augustine *Serm.* 272.

in the eucharist we are offered in and with Christ, and only so can we offer Christ. Writer after writer follows St. Cyprian in seeing this principle symbolized in the fact that the bread and wine, which are to become Christ's body and blood, are made up of many grains or berries brought into one: or again in the fact that water is added to the wine to represent the addition of the people to Christ in the sacrifice. "For if we should offer wine alone, then the blood of Christ begins to be separated from us; but if it be water alone, then the people begin to be separated from Him; but when both are mingled, . . . then is it a spiritual and heavenly sacrament."[1] The idea that the church must be offered in Christ appears in the liturgies—for example, in the prayer of the Leonine Sacramentary "that God would propitiously sanctify the church's gifts, and, accepting the oblation of their spiritual sacrifice, would make the worshippers themselves an eternal offering to Him."[2] It recurs constantly in

[1] Cyprian *Ep.* lxiii. 13, and Thomassin *l.c.* cap. xix. 8, 9.
[2] *P. L.* lv. 40 "nosmet ipsos tibi perfice munus aeternum."

writers of many epochs.[1] But it is identified with St. Augustine as with no one else.

That great father of course recognizes that what is presented in the eucharist is "the sacrifice of our ransom," "the sacrifice of the body and blood of Christ."[2] But the whole of his emphasis is laid upon the fact that we are joined to Him in one body, that not without ourselves can we offer Christ, that the "body" which is represented in the bread, and which is offered upon the altar, is, in Christ, also the church. "The bread which you see on the altar," he says to the children, "sanctified by the word of God, is the body of Christ. The cup, or rather what the cup contains, sanctified by the word of God, is the blood of Christ. By means of these things Christ our Lord willed to offer us His body and the blood which He shed for us for the remission of sins. If you have received well, you are

---

[1] *Cf.* Optatus and Gregory, pp. 92, 303.

[2] *Confess.* ix. 12 (32), *de an. et ej. orig.* i. 10, 13, iv. 38. But here he is arguing, "You cannot offer the body of Christ except for those who are His members."

what you have received. . . . He willed that we ourselves should be His sacrifice." The thought recurs frequently in his great work *On the City of God*. "The whole redeemed city, that is the congregation or society of the saints, is offered as a universal sacrifice to God by the High Priest, Who offered nothing less than Himself in suffering for us, so that we might become the body of so glorious a head, in that 'form of a servant' (our human nature) which He had taken. For it was this that He offered, in this that He was offered, as it is in virtue of this (His humanity) that He is mediator, priest, and sacrifice." Then, after a reference to St. Paul's words about presenting our bodies a living sacrifice, he continues: "This is the Christian sacrifice: the 'many' become 'one body in Christ.' And it is this that the church celebrates by means of the sacrament of the altar, familiar to the faithful, where it is shown to her that in what she offers, she herself is offered." Again, of Christ's perfect sacrifice of Himself, "He willed the church's sacrifice to be a daily sacrament.

For as she is the body of Him the head, she learns through Him to offer up herself." Again, "God's most glorious and best sacrifice is we ourselves, that is His city, of which we celebrate the mystery in our oblations which are known to the faithful." Once more, arguing that the eucharistic sacrifice cannot be offered *to* the martyrs, he says: "The sacrifice itself is the body of Christ, which is not offered to them, for they themselves are it."[1]

And it is plain enough that this doctrine of the church herself being the sacrifice of the altar, as offered there in and with Christ, brings us back to the fundamentally Christian point of view, that the only acceptable sacrifices of the new law are the sacrifices of persons, and of things or rites only as adjuncts or expressions of persons. "The sacrifice"—again to quote Augustine—"is the man consecrated and devoted to God, dying to the world that he may live to God."

In its most characteristic and historical

[1] Aug. *Serm.* 227, *de civ. Dei*, x. 6, 20, xix. 23, xxii. 10.

sense, indeed, sacrifice is a corporate act of many persons — a nation or a church. And such corporate acts must needs be external. But, all the same, the outward sacrifice is valueless unless it be "in spirit and in truth"—unless, that is, it be the sacrifice of persons. "The visible sacrifice is the sacrament or sacred sign of the invisible —that is, of what goes on in us"—the movement of human wills towards God, and behind all and in all, of Christ offering to the Father our manhood perfected in Him.[1]

[1] *De civ. Dei*, x. 5, 6.

§ 4. *Summary.*

Now we are in position to answer the question as to the sense in which the Church of the first four or five centuries understood the eucharistic sacrifice—leaving room for individual variations—in some such summary as this.

First of all, the eucharist is a sacrifice because in it the Christian church — the great priestly body, and "soul of the world" — exercises her privilege of sonship in free approach to the Father in the name of Christ. She comes before the Father with her material offerings of bread and wine, and of those things wherein God has prospered her, bearing witness that all good things come of Him; and though He needs nothing from man, yet He accepts the recognition of His fatherhood from loyal and free hearts. She comes with her wide-spreading intercessions for

SUMMARY.

the whole race of mankind,[1] and for her members living and departed. She offers her glad sacrifice of praise and thanksgiving for all the blessings of creation and redemption. She solemnly commemorates the passion in word and in symbolic action, through the bread broken and the wine outpoured, the appointed tokens of Christ's sacrificed body and blood, reciting before God His own words and acts in instituting the holy eucharist. This is the church's sacrifice; and it is all that she can do. She can but make the appointed remembrance of Christ's passion and death and resurrection and of His second coming which she awaits, and offer to the Father the appointed

[1] St. Augustine has been referred to above (p. 206) as declaring that it was no practice of the church to offer for any except those who belong to the church. Elsewhere he takes a broader line (*Ep.* 217, 2), and asserts that the church does pray for those outside at the altar. And this was the fact: see Bp. Wordsworth *Holy Communion* (Parker, 1891), pp. 63 ff. and Epiphanius quoted in Brightman, p. 469, n. 13. But St. Thomas (*S. Th.* p. iii. qu. lxxix. art. 7) accepts Augustine's first position, and adds: "Wherefore also in the canon of the mass there is no prayer for those who are outside the church."

symbols, praying Him by the consecrating power of the Holy Ghost to fill the sacrifice with a divine power by accepting the earthly elements at the heavenly altar. Then is the time for God's response to the church's uplifting of her heart and gifts; and He by His Spirit consecrates the gifts to be, in the midst of the worshipping church, the body and blood of the Lord.

Now the eucharist is a sacrifice in a second and deeper sense, for God has united the offerings of the church to the ever-living sacrifice of the great High Priest in the heavenly sanctuary, or has given His presence among them who is their propitiation and their spiritual food.

Then once more, united afresh in one body to God by the communion in Christ's body and blood, the church offers herself, one with Christ as a body with its head, living in the same life and indwelt by the same Spirit: she offers herself that her whole fellowship, both the living and the dead, having their sins forgiven through the propitiation of Christ, may be accepted with all their good works and prayers "in the beloved." And in the self-oblation of the church is the culmination of the sacrifice.

The sacrifice is the sacrifice of the whole body, and the communion is the communion of the whole body. The celebrating priest is indeed the necessary organ of the body's action. He is the mouth with which she prays, and the hand by which she offers and blesses in the name of Christ. But the sacrifice is the church's sacrifice. "*We* bless the cup," "*we* break the bread," St. Paul says. "We offer," "we do sacrifice," is the language of the liturgies.[1] "No priest," says Peter Lombard, "says 'I offer,' but 'we offer,' in the person of the whole church."[2] Again in the gift communicated all are on a level. The utmost that God can give—the very being of His own Son—is given to all alike to bind them all together in one divine and human life. "Sometimes," says

[1] Brightman *l.c.* p. 20, 53, 133, 190: and in the Roman canon, "offerimus," "meam ac vestrum sacrificium," "oblationem . . . cunctae familiae tuae," etc.

[2] *Sentt.* iv. 13.

St. Chrysostom, "there is no difference between priest and people; for example, when we partake of the awful mysteries. (It is not as under the old covenant) for all alike are given the same things: for all it is one bread which lies in view, and one cup."[1]

[1] Chrys. *in ii. Cor. Hom.* xviii. (*P. G.* lxi. 527). The whole passage is apposite.

CHAPTER IV.

OUR AUTHORITIES.

§ 1. *Mediæval authority*.

THROUGHOUT the argument of the previous chapters the appeal has been mainly to the mind of the church, and especially to the mind of the ancient church, on the subject of the eucharist. The inquiry has disclosed appreciable differences in the eucharistic teaching of the ancient fathers: a different tone of teaching in the early Alexandrians, Clement and Origen, as compared with Irenæus and Cyprian; and in the great Greek theologians, St. Gregory and St. Chrysostom, as compared with St. Augustine. It has disclosed variation and ambiguity, and one-sided tendencies in opposite directions in certain early schools of thought; but on the whole, and behind these differences, a clear tradition of belief about the eucharist has been apparent which has the best title to be called catholic. And it is to this normal ancient tradition that the primary appeal has been made. I want to find myself, in the church in England, now in the twentieth century, of one mind across the ages with the ancient Christian church. Beyond this it will remain for me to make good my appeal to the ultimate authority, the books of the New Testament. But before doing this, the ground must be secured from the objections which will make themselves heard from two sides.

I have not appealed to the theologians of the Reformation, whether English or foreign, as if their views on any matter could be taken to represent a settlement of the question; and I have also found myself unable to rest in the mediæval positions. It has appeared plainly enough that, with regard both to the doctrine of the gift given to us by God in Holy Communion and to that of the sacrifice there offered, some specially characteristic elements in the teaching of the West in the middle ages and later period will have to be abandoned.

Indeed it is not too much to say that if the development of eucharistic teaching and practice in the church, from the time of St. Cyril and St. Chrysostom in the East, and from that of St. Augustine and his followers in the West, down nearly to our own time, were to be obliterated, hardly anything that is valuable would have been lost, and a great deal that is a most serious hindrance and cause of division would have dropped out.

But though this appeal to ancient teaching is characteristically Anglican, there are those among us who, both from the Protestant and from the Catholic side, are dissatisfied with it; and I will endeavour to deal first with those who would plead that sufficient respect has not been shown to mediæval authority.

On the ground of free historical examination the early mediæval development of eucharistic teaching in the East appears to have been coloured by a seriously monophysite tendency—a tendency, that is, to represent the supernatural and the divine as absorbing and annihilating the natural and the human which it uses as its vehicle. It is also indisputable, that when this tendency reached the West and superseded, on the subject of the eucharist, St. Augustine's hitherto dominant influence, it coalesced with a markedly superstitious and irrational spirit in the church; and that it was in the atmosphere thus generated that the doctrine of transubstantiation secured its ground in its original form. Thus even if later scholastic theology had succeeded more completely than in fact was the case, in remedying the faults of the original doctrine, the term, as a dogmatic definition, would remain as a pure mistake, the legacy of a deplorable moment in church history.

On the subject of the eucharistic sacrifice there was almost no intellectual inquiry in the middle ages or up to the time of the Reformation: but the phrasing of the Tridentine dogma as to a sacrifice "propitiatory in the true sense" offered in the mass;[1] the teaching that it is through the sacrifice offered

[1] Sess. xxii. capp. 1. 2; "vere propitiatorium"; *cf.* above, pp. 176 ff., and app. note 14, p. 305.

by the priests of the church on earth that Christ realizes His priesthood after the order of Melchizedek; and the complete obliteration from view in this connection of the heavenly intercession and self-presentation of Christ, which had been so prominent in the patristic theology—all this prepared the way for what has become the perilously dominant tendency of speculation about the sacrifice in the later Roman church. Thus on the subject both of the gift and of the sacrifice, the eucharistic development of the middle ages, as compared with the less formulated teaching and belief of the early church, represents loss and not gain, deterioration and not advance.

But occasionally, even among Anglicans, our right thus to go back behind the authority of the mediæval church is vigorously challenged. "The authority of the church in the thirteenth or sixteenth centuries," we are told, "is identical with its authority in the fourth or third." To this I should reply, first, that there is no decision of the whole church of any period about the eucharist such as in any way corresponds in weight to the decrees of the general councils, for example, about our Lord's person. In fact, without attempting to estimate precisely to what sort of belief, as to a change in the bread and wine, the orthodox East is committed,[1] it is doubtful whether there has been any period subsequent to the division of East and West when they could have been brought to an agreement on the subject of the presence or the sacrifice, even if they had consented to meet in fair and open synod on the ancient terms. And secondly, I should reply that the tone of church authority in the middle ages becomes so changed; its abandonment of ancient safeguards or limitations becomes so marked; that—especially in the absence of any formal canonical decree—it loses weight as authority almost altogether.

The lesson which we are intended to learn from the church of the old covenant appears to be that a real religious authority admits of being so much misused as to become com-

[1] See, however, an admirable paper by Mr. Birkbeck in *Report of Round Table Conference*, p. 15.

pletely misleading. The Scribes and Pharisees who sat in Moses' seat had, according to our Lord, a real authority. He would have it recognized and obeyed by His disciples. But their whole tone and teaching had developed along a false and narrow line. It had practically ceased to represent the spirit of ancient prophecy. They had "taken away the key of knowledge." They had "made the word of God of none effect because of their tradition." Thus the ecclesiastical authorities in the church of the old covenant did, in effect, reject the Christ, for whose coming they existed to prepare a people.

Now though this misuse of ecclesiastical authority was under our Lord's eyes all the time, He deliberately reinstituted ecclesiastical authority in the church of the new covenant. One of His perfections is the total absence in His manhood of the undue influence of reaction. He gave then to His church a renewed lease of authority to bind and loose—that is, to legislate—which has been accepted as applicable to doctrine as well as to practice. But the deplorable failure of the ecclesiastical authority of the old covenant to accomplish the end for which it existed ought to have acted as a much more serious warning to the authority of the new than in fact, at some periods, it has shown itself to be. It ought to have made it a first instinct with the bishops of all ages to be on their guard against gradual departures from the original spirit of Christian prophecy. It ought—to put the matter in definite terms—to have made them specially careful to maintain the constant appeal to Scripture, the record of the first inspired pattern of teaching, which the church exists to guard and to perpetuate, but to which it has no authority to add.

Now the ancient church did faithfully and continually recur to this pattern, and faithfully recognized the limitation of its function. It is evident how constant is the effect of the scriptural pattern, on which they are mainly occupied in commenting, in moulding and restraining the teaching of Origen and Chrysostom and Augustine. The appeal to Scripture is explicit and constant. These fathers knew that they existed simply to maintain a once-given teaching, and that the justification of any dogma was simply the necessity for guarding the faith once for all delivered and recorded. There can be no doubt of their point of view.[1] But when we turn to the period which fixed on the western church the dogma of transubstantiation, all is changed. The specific appeal to the scriptures of the New Testament to verify or correct current tendencies is gone. The scriptures, so far as they are referred to, are merged in a miscellaneous mass of authorities.[2] The safeguard has vanished.

In regard to this particular dogma it cannot be plausibly argued, either that it represents the view of the fathers, or that it —as distinct from any other view of the real presence—was necessary to safeguard the original position. There is nothing in the New Testament even to suggest the vanishing of the original substances. The more it is examined, the more clearly it appears that

[1] I have sought to show this in *Roman Catholic Claims* (Longmans, 1900), chap. 3. [2] *Dissertations*, p. 250.

this dogma, at least, was arrived at by the authorities of the church through the neglect of all those precautions and safeguards which a true idea of church authority, and a true appreciation of its dangers, would have suggested, and which in patristic days were so abundantly observed. Or again, no one can maintain, with any degree of plausibility, that a doctrine of Christ's priesthood after the order of Melchizedek which neglects to put His presentation of Himself in heaven in the first place, can find in the New Testament any degree of confirmation.

Now Christ has guaranteed the permanence in the world of the grace and truth which came by Him. But He never came near to guaranteeing His church against misuses of ecclesiastical authority akin to those which rendered the scribes and Pharisees and chief priests so wholly inadequate for the fulfilment of their divine function. Thus, when we see the authorities of the Christian church at any period ignoring the real appeal to Scripture as at once the motive and the limit of their dogmatic action, we are much more than justified in appealing back behind them to that on which we all alike rest—the foundation of the apostles and prophets. And if we find cause to mistrust ecclesiastical authority in a few instances, this tends to modify our whole attitude towards it. It comes to occupy a place in our minds—in our whole idea of religion and the church — proportionate to that which it appears to occupy in the mind and teaching of Christ—that is to say, we recognize its reality and its function in the order of the church; but we can never regard it as absolute or final, except when it can justify its action or utterance by the appeal behind itself to the word of God — the record of the original apostolic teaching.

But it is important to remember that, though the mediæval church overlaid the really catholic traditions with some misleading accretions, and though we must claim our freedom to treat them as accretions, yet none the less the underlying substance of its teaching as to the individual and social meaning of Holy Communion and as to the presenting before God of the one sacrifice, remained what it had ever been in the church. It required purging but not reversing.[1]

---

[1] In the eucharistic teaching of some mediæval writers there is very little of these accretions at all: for instance, in so late an author as Raymund of Sabunde.

§ 2. *The authority of the reformation.*

What has been said of the mediæval authority is at least as true of the authority of the Reformation theology, and of the special type of Reformation theology which was characteristic of the English church. It cannot be taken by itself as constituting our standard or court of appeal.

No doubt we in the Anglican church have contracted certain specific obligations, doctrinal and ceremonial, with regard to the eucharist, by which we are unmistakably bound. But the principle of authority to which the Anglican church has almost consistently appealed is the very one which it is the object of this book to emphasize. The Convocation of 1571, which imposed upon the clergy subscription to the Articles of Religion, issued a canon to preachers enjoining them to "teach nothing in their sermons which they should require to be devoutly held or believed by the people, except what is agreeable to the doctrine of the Old or New Testament, and what the catholic fathers and ancient bishops have collected out of the said doctrine."[1] And the formal appeal of the Anglican divines has always been to the *quod semper*, *quod ubique*, *quod ab omnibus*, as well as to Scripture.

But on the subject of the eucharist in particular it required time before this general appeal could be made good in detail. Meanwhile reaction from Rome was the dominant tendency, and reaction is seldom well balanced. It must be obvious to any one reading our divines of the sixteenth or seventeenth centuries that it is often extremely difficult to ascertain their positive teaching —except, perhaps, in the case of Hooker; or to reconcile what they assert positively at one time with what they say by way of rejection of Roman doctrine at another; or again, to reconcile them among themselves. The phrase, the "Reformation settlement," expresses well enough a provisional arrange-

[1] Cardwell *Synodalia*, i. p. 126.

ment or compromise arrived at to enable the Anglican church to go on working but "settlement" is the last word one would choose to describe the general condition of the Reformation theology.

Thus I am content to prove that nothing in what has been said about the eucharist in the preceding chapters is inconsistent with any positive or negative declaration of the Anglican authorities; while on the other hand it is my main contention that it is the fullest and frankest expression of that mind of the fathers to which the Anglican Church consistently appeals.

There is nothing, then, in the doctrine of the eucharist as expressed above which is inconsistent with Anglican formulas.

(1) As to the substance of the eucharistic gift (chap. ii. § 1) I have but restated and developed the theology of Hooker, who so richly and profoundly reasserts the teaching which came from the great doctors of the incarnation in the fourth and fifth centuries. And again it is wholly agreeable to the language of our authoritative formulas. Thus

in them it is declared that the "inward and spiritual grace" of the Lord's supper is the "body and blood of Christ which are verily and indeed taken and received by the faithful:"[1] that Christ is "our spiritual food and sustenance in that holy sacrament," that "banquet of most heavenly food."[2] And this "body" of Christ is identified with His "flesh," and associated with His whole person; we "spiritually eat the flesh of Christ, and drink His blood; we dwell in Christ and Christ in us; we are one with Christ and Christ with us."[3] And by this eating we are no less incorporated with one another, in "the mystical body, which is the blessed company of all faithful people," than into Christ Himself.[4]

(2) The teaching of the objective presence (as explained above, chap. ii. § 2) of the body and blood of Christ, and so of Christ Himself, as sacramentally identified with the consecrated elements—the teaching that the

[1] Catechism.
[2] Exhortations i. and ii. in the Communion Service.
[3] Exhortation iii. and Prayer of Humble Access.
[4] Prayer i. after Communion.

bread and wine are themselves consecrated to be, prior to reception, spiritually and really the body and blood of Christ—is at least allowed doctrine according to the Anglican formulas. The objectiveness of the presence in this sense is indeed at least suggested by their language in several places. Thus in the Catechism it is to be noticed that, whereas in dealing with baptism there are only two questions and answers, one as to the "outward visible sign or form," and the second as to "the inward and spiritual grace"; in dealing with the eucharist there are three: one as to "the outward part or sign," another as to "the inward part or thing signified," and a third as to "the benefits of partaking." And this difference certainly suggests a distinction, applicable to the eucharist but not to baptism, between the *res sacramenti*, or its inward reality, and the *virtus*, or moral effect of receiving it worthily.[1] In the eucharist then, the Catechism suggests, there is an invisible thing, given to us in order to be received, but itself

[1] *Cf.* Raymund of Sabunde *op. cit.* tit. 286.

present in the sacrament before reception. This is the "ghostly substance" of the sacrament, spoken of in the homily "of the worthy receiving and reverent esteeming of the sacrament of the body and blood of Christ."[1] And again, in the 28th article, the body of Christ is said to be "given" and "taken," as well as "eaten," though, as all would admit, "only after an heavenly and spiritual manner."

We must admit, on the other hand, that the doctrine of the objective presence in, under, or with, the consecrated elements is plainly evaded and not asserted in the revised Declaration about kneeling appended to the Communion Service in 1662;[2] and, what is more important, it is evaded by the special turn given in the form of consecration to the

[1] This appears to be the true reading, rather than "ghostly sustenance": see *The Witness of the Homilies* (S.P.C.K. 1900), p. 37 — a publication of the Church Historical Society.

[2] Which, however, *was* revised so as to condemn the belief in a "corporal presence of Christ's natural flesh and blood" such as exists in heaven (which the Romanists also reject), instead of condemning the belief in a "real and essential presence."

prayer for the blessing of the elements. This now runs, not as in the first Prayer Book of Edward VI.—"with Thy Holy Spirit and word vouchsafe to bless and sanctify these Thy gifts and creatures of bread and wine that they may be unto us the body and blood of Thy most dearly beloved Son Jesus Christ"—a form completely in accordance with most ancient precedents; but "grant that *we receiving these Thy creatures* of bread and wine . . . may be partakers of His most blessed body and blood." And this, though it is not far removed from some ancient forms already referred to,[1] certainly does evade the question of the effect of consecration upon the elements themselves.

It appears to be therefore certain that Hooker would still be justified, as far as the Anglican standards taken by themselves are concerned—even since the revision of the Prayer Book in 1662—in seeking to shelve the question of any presence in the elements apart from the act of receiving; and that even Waterland, in going further and denying

[1] See above, pp. 82 f.

any such presence, was not transgressing the limits of allowed opinion: but no one, on the other hand, is justified in denying to others the right to hold and teach what is the accepted doctrine of the ancient church as to an objective presence prior to the act of reception and independent of it.

This conclusion, that our present formulas leave the question of the objectiveness of the presence an open one, so that we are not justified in calling one another heretics for holding or denying it, commanded the assent of John Keble;[1] who moreover justified this open position by the absence of any really catholic decision on the subject. And the same conclusion has recently been clearly reaffirmed in the Archbishop of Canterbury's charge.[2] It is, however, surely unfortunate that the Archbishop identified the objective

---

[1] Keble's *Spiritual Letters* (Parker, 1885), cxviii—cxxi. Keble also thought that the questions of what exactly the wicked eat and drink, and whether "the whole Christ" is present "in each particle *of either kind*," were left open questions.

[2] Charge delivered at his first visitation by Frederick, Archbishop of Canterbury (Macmillan, 1898), p. 10.

doctrine as Luther's view, for Luther's view —called consubstantiation by its opponents —is a very ambiguous matter; and if he held such a view as is expressed in this book, it was no more *his* view than the doctrine of the incarnation can be called his doctrine because he held it. The ancient church held the doctrine of a real presence without transubstantiation; and it is to antiquity that the Church of England makes her appeal.

(3) It will not be denied that in rejecting the doctrine of transubstantiation (chap. ii. § 3) in the form in which it best deserves that name, and in which it "overthroweth the nature of a sacrament," we are supported by the Anglican article and tradition.

(4) It will also hardly be denied that what has been said about the meaning of a spiritual presence (chap. ii. § 4) is thoroughly in accordance with Anglican language. There is a passage in Jeremy Taylor[1] in which he contrasts two meanings of the word spiritual as applied to the eucharistic presence:

[1] *Real Presence*, sect. 1, 8.

(*a*) the presence of the body after the manner of a spirit, and (*b*) a presence to our spirits only; and he declares only the latter to be what "we [Anglicans] mean." But the latter explanation proves to be highly ambiguous when analysed, because, as already shown, subject and object cannot be thus put in contrast to one another; and also it is not congenial to the language of the Prayer Book. The Prayer Book language suggests a real gift given by God to us which in its own nature is spiritual and heavenly, and which, for that very reason, only believing spirits can appreciate and appropriate. As to the relation of the gift given to the faith of the receiver, a preference has been confessed above for the Augustinian language recited in the body of the 29th article over the more sharply defined mediæval language.

(5) On the subject of the eucharistic sacrifice our 31st article only excludes any treatment of it which in any way suggests the insufficiency of the one offering of Christ, and of such a suggestion the treatment of it in this book (chap. iii. § 2) could not be

accused. Beyond this our formulas are silent. Under the influence of reaction, in our later Prayer Books there was an unfortunate suppression of the ancient language of the commemorative oblation. The address to the Father — " Therefore, O Lord and heavenly Father, according to the institution of Thy dearly beloved Son, our Saviour Jesus Christ, we Thy humble servants do celebrate, and make here before Thy divine Majesty, with these Thy holy gifts, the memorial which Thy Son has willed us to make, having in remembrance His blessed passion, mighty resurrection, and glorious ascension"—which was retained in Edward's first Prayer Book, and which has recovered its place in the Prayer Books of the Scottish and American churches of our communion, has unhappily vanished. But we still recite the words and acts of Christ's institution before God as part of a prayer, and not before men as an instruction; and the rich prayer of oblation which follows the communion and the Lord's Prayer admirably expresses what to the mind of St. Augustine was the culminating point in the eucharistic sacrifice.

The estimate just made of the positive teaching of the present Anglican formularies no doubt compels the admission that they fall somewhat short of the ancient language. But they reject no authoritative formula of the whole church, and they appeal behind themselves to ancient consent. We ought not to interpret antiquity or force its meaning from the point of view of our present formularies; but, abiding by their positive requirements and limitations, to read them in the light of "the catholic fathers and ancient bishops." That, I submit, is the most truly Anglican method.

§ 3. *The authority of the church at large.*

In what has been said above, it is the ultimate authority of which I have been speaking. No doubt for an ordinary private Christian it is enough to follow the guidance of the authority of his own part of the church, as he can read it in plain documents, as it is interpreted and made alive for him by the pastors whom the providence of God has given him to feed him with the divine word, and as his own private study of the sacred scriptures can further enlighten him. But there is a special vocation for scholars, and this vocation lies in great part in purging the current tradition, or enlarging it, by perpetual recurrence to the divine originals. Thus the real security of a church, as against the constant tendency to doctrinal deterioration, lies in giving free scope to this the scholar's " gift of knowledge ": and the requirement which this lays upon the ordinary members of the church is that they should be ready to mortify the desire (so natural to human laziness) to be exempted from the moral and spiritual trouble involved in relearning old truths in a completer or purer form, and so taking their part in "testing all things" and "holding fast that which is good." For in fact no church is ever safe unless in its whole bulk, and by the spiritual labour of minds of every kind of quality, it is perpetually undergoing what—by an application of a biological term with a somewhat changed intention—we may call "reversion to type," the perennial "type," or pattern of apostolic teaching.

The student, then, especially where, as on the subject of the eucharist, he has to deal with a doctrine which has never become matter of ecumenical definition, will be perpetually comparing the existing teaching of a church, or school of theology, with the teaching of past ages, to see whether it is not in need of revision—whether forgotten elements and aspects of the truth have not to be recovered, or deteriorations and accretions

CATHOLIC AUTHORITY. 241

noted and corrected or banished. But this very process will only increase his sense of the reality of a catholic tradition about the eucharist—a teaching really universal and original—which is most plainly discerned in the ancient and undivided church; and for this he will claim, with all reason, the greatest deference. All reason demands that the New Testament should be read in the light of this ancient catholic tradition. For in fact nothing is more certain than that a sound historical criticism will not allow us to tear the New Testament documents out of the heart of the first Christian literature as a whole. These documents indeed bear it upon their faces that they presuppose the existence of a church tradition and that they are written, not to give primary instruction in Christian principles, but to enlighten and correct those who had already inherited the common elementary teaching.[1] This does not mean that we are to force the meaning

[1] See Luke i. 1—4, 1 Cor. xi. 2, 23, xv. 1, 2, Gal. i. 8, 9, 2 Thess. iii. 6, Hebr. vi. 1, 2, James i. 19, 1 John ii. 24, 27, Jude 3.

of the New Testament. But it does mean that the common and original mind of the church is to give us our point of view in approaching the Scriptures, and that we are far more likely to be right if we approach them in this way than if we merely approach them as isolated "documents." They represent the mind of the church at its best and freshest: they represent the utterance of its highest inspiration: but none the less the spirit of the church as a whole is the same spirit which inspired the apostles, and is far more likely than any isolated point of view —any "private interpretation"—to give us the clue to their meaning. We come back always to approve the reasonableness of the old formula—the church to teach, the Bible to prove.

§ 4. *The test of scripture.*

Does the New Testament then verify the account of the eucharist which has been given in the earlier chapters of this book? And, first, does it verify the account of the nature of the gift of God therein given?

(1) That the eucharist is the divinely provided occasion for realizing the relationship to our Lord described in the sixth chapter of St. John—for eating the flesh of the living Christ and drinking His blood, and so receiving Christ in His whole person into ourselves, to abide in us that we may abide in Him—is the natural, and the most widely accepted, conclusion, from the language of the New Testament. The only important argument against it is that the word used in the accounts of its institution, and therefore also in the liturgical language which follows them, is "body," not "flesh"; and accordingly some of recent years have,

with more or less distinctness, interpreted "this is my body" to mean that this loaf which is broken and distributed, is or represents the church, which is Christ's body, the many members sharing a single life.

Now in a certain sense this is true. St. Augustine teaches that what we receive in the eucharist is the flesh of Christ, which is also called His body: and that by the flesh or body of Christ received, we, the many, become one body in Christ. And, as has been already said, St. Augustine would refuse to draw a sharp line of separation between Christ's "own" body and the church. The church, in Him, becomes His own body. And this truth he would emphasize to the uttermost: "We become," he says, "what we receive." In a real sense, but using rather extreme language, he even says that the inner part or thing signified in the eucharist is the church.[1] But it is this secondarily, because primarily it is Christ's own flesh. The word "flesh" describes, we

---

[1] See *Serm.* 227, 272, and above, p. 206. Rupert of Deutz (*P. L.* clxix. 182—3) discusses this view excellently.

may say, the principle of His manhood in a more abstract form. "This is my body" describes it as presented in concrete reality. But His "body" no less than His flesh means the manhood of His own person first of all. And St. Paul's expression about "not discerning the body," means primarily not discerning Christ's own personal manhood given us in the sacrament.

What seems to me to make this certain is that just as Christ's "flesh" in St. John vi. is coupled with His "blood"—His manhood with His life—so the eucharistic "body" is coupled with the "blood": and this must mean that the primary reference of the latter as well as the former pair of terms is to elements in Christ's own person. For "the blood" of Christ in the New Testament language receives no extension of meaning such as is given to "the body": it means only Christ's own life as offered through death and so rendered efficacious to save and to quicken His brethren.

Thus when St. Paul says that "the bread which we break" is "a communion of (or

' in ') the body of Christ," no doubt the word "communion" is not precisely identical with "communication," but it implies it. It is only because the bread first of all is Christ's own body, that we by sharing it together have one fellowship in that holy unity.[1]

(2) When we examine into the belief of the church in an objective body and blood of Christ sacramentally identified with the bread and wine, we find it to have been simply due to our Lord's language, reinforced by St. Paul's. Our Lord said, "This *is* my body—my blood." It *is*, I venture to think, useless to argue with too great exactness about the word *is*. It describes very various kinds of identification. It is a sufficient warning against laying too much stress upon it, that in one report our Lord is made to say, "This [cup] *is*," not "my blood," but "the new covenant in my blood." The copula, therefore, is clearly indeterminate. But the language used certainly suggests what the Church has believed, that the spiritual gifts of Christ's body and

[1] 1 Cor. x. 16: contrast *Did.* ix. 4, see p. 325.

blood are identified with the elements, as blessed and consecrated, before they are given to the receivers; and St. Paul's language of stern instruction to the irreverent and selfish communicants at Corinth—that they eat and drink judgment to themselves, because in the outward elements they do not "discern" their spiritual counterpart, suggests the same conclusion. The New Testament at least confirms the church's belief.

(3) Again nothing in the New Testament suggests transubstantiation. "This (bread) is my body: this (wine) is my blood,"[1] suggests some sort of identification of certain things—bread and wine—with certain other things of a higher order, viz., Christ's body and blood; but it does not suggest that these natural objects in any sense cease to exist. I will not urge, in accordance with St. Matthew and St. Mark's

[1] Certainly among the most wearisome pages in theology are those filled with the discussion of these words by Romanist theologians. Do they mean "This bread (or wine) becomes at this moment by transubstantiation My body (or blood)"—or what precisely? *Ex hypothesi* they cannot be at once both bread and Christ's body, both wine and Christ's blood.

account, that our Lord, after the wine had been declared to be His blood, still spoke of it as "this fruit of the vine"; for St. Luke's account, taking into consideration the doubt about the text, is at least ambiguous.[1] But St. Paul has no hesitation in calling the bread, after it had been blessed, "this bread"—or saying, "there is one bread."[2]

(4) What was said above, in attempted correction of some later tendencies in eucharistic theology, about the meaning of a spiritual presence, as involving subservience to a divine purpose, was expressly grounded on New Testament language. And certainly the purpose of the eucharistic gifts, as represented in the New Testament, is exclusively what has been maintained above—that they may be partaken of. And if some doubts were expressed as to the justification of saying explicitly and certainly that those who are wholly faithless do receive, though they do not benefit by, the body and blood

---

[1] See Luke xxii. 18—20, Matt. xxvi. 28—9, Mk. xiv. 24—5; cf. p. 311. [2] 1 Cor. x. 17, xi. 28.

of Christ, that was because St. John's language, in reporting our Lord, certainly implies, as to His flesh and blood, that only those who have faith can eat and drink them.

I should contend, therefore, that a doctrine of the Real Presence, such as is maintained in this book, at least gives a natural interpretation to the whole language of the New Testament and is in conflict with none of it.

But no doubt there is some justification at first sight for saying that the New Testament does not suggest that the eucharist is a sacrifice.

(5) The doctrine of the sacrifice of the eucharist was found above (chap. iv.) to involve, first of all, a sacrifice—of prayers and offerings, and thankful commemorations and symbolical rites—made by the church on earth. But the consecration of the earthly elements of bread and wine, in accordance with the institution of Christ our high priest, to become the body and blood of His own sacrifice, for the reception of the faithful—this was found to translate

the church's earthly sacrifice into a region of higher power: it becomes identified with Christ's heavenly offering; it is exalted in Him to the heavenly places, and accepted through Him by the Father.

The enquiry then into the scriptural basis of this doctrine involves two chief points: (a) Is the doctrine of Christ, as our perpetual high priest in the heavenly court, interceding for us in the power and merits of a once made sacrifice, scriptural? And (b) is there scriptural ground for saying that in the eucharist in a special and pre-eminent degree we are brought into union with Christ as our eternal priest and sacrifice?

(a) Now, as to the first point, our appeal is primarily to the Epistle to the Hebrews, an epistle written by an unknown hand in the apostolic circle, and perhaps we may say specially in the circle of St. Paul, before the destruction of Jerusalem; an epistle already cited by Clement, in the subapostolic generation, as a document of authority on which he models his thought and language. It is, in fact, in a unique sense the primary authority for the doctrine of Christ's priesthood, which is nowhere else in the New Testament so explicitly stated; and it is of special importance for the doctrine of the eucharist because it is, as has been already remarked,[1] the only one of the writings of the New Testament in which our religion is considered as a covenant of worship—under which all the imperfect principles of ritual which belonged to the old covenant are realized in the perfected church, the church which, even here and now, belongs to the world to come, and the institutions of heaven.[2]

Plainly then in this epistle the central idea is that the Son of God was made man to qualify Himself by human sympathies for human priesthood; and that in our manhood He suffered death—He must needs have suffered it—for the perfecting of His human sympathy with pain,[3] for the fulfilment of His obedience to the Father's will,[4] to accomplish the victory over our tyrant Satan

[1] See p. 167, and A. B. Davidson's *Hebrews*, pp. 196—7.
[2] Hebr. vi. 4—5, ix. 11, 23.
[3] ii. 10, 17.   [4] v. 8, x. 9—10.

through that which had been his chief instrument of enslavement,[1] and finally because death was the penalty of sin and the shedding of blood the legal cost of remission.[2] Now in suffering death the Son made in our nature an offering of Himself, and this His act of offering Himself is sometimes apparently attached, even in this epistle, specially to the moment of death, which was the moral crisis of self-sacrifice;[3] but the dominant point of view is based upon the sacrificial ritual of the day of atonement. There the moment of offering and of atonement was not the moment of the slaying of the victim, but that of the entrance of the high priest with the blood of the victims into the most holy place to sprinkle it upon the mercy seat.[4] Accordingly in the Epistle to the Hebrews all that goes before the ascension is the preparation of Christ for His priestly work. His work as the great high priest, and His entrance into at least the effectiveness of His office, begins with His entrance

[1] Hebr. ii. 14.   [2] ix. 15.
[3] x. 10.   [4] ix. 7.

into the true holy of holies, in the power of His own blood once for all surrendered in death.[1] In the power of that once made sacrifice, once made in "eternal spirit," and now become eternally effective in the indissoluble life of His resurrection, and lifted into the heavenly places in the glory of His ascension, He presents Himself for us, our intercessor, our eternal king-priest after the order of Melchizedek. It is at His entrance into heaven, and not upon the cross, that He accomplishes His atonement for us, according to the Epistle to the Hebrews; and His work as high priest, which begins with His entrance into heaven, is perpetual. His propitiation and His intercession are identical: and both consist in His "appearing" or presenting Himself for us. Or, as it may be ritually described, they consist in the sprinkling of the blood; for "the blood of sprinkling" (which is only an expression for the permanent efficacy of the sacrifice and priesthood) is, as well as "Jesus the mediator," represented as among the abiding

[1] Davidson *op. cit.*, pp. 150 ff., 196 ff.

objects of the heavenly place to which already we have been brought near.[1]

The ideas of the author of this epistle have had strange violence done to them, because the speciality of his point of view, as compared to that of the other New Testament writers, has not been observed. It is true of St. John to say (with Dr. Westcott) that "the simple idea of the death of Christ, as separated from His life, falls wholly into the background."[2] With him, too, our "advocate" and "propitiation" is one who died indeed, but is alive for evermore—the "Lamb as it had been slain."[3] But it is even more conspicuously true of the author of this epistle. The death with him is part of the preparation of the high priest to fulfil His sacrificial ministry in heaven in the power of an indissoluble life, human as well as divine: "ever living to make intercession for us," a priest for ever after the order of

[1] See, on this whole paragraph, ii. 17—18 (where the suffering is viewed as past), iv. 14, v. 6—10, vi. 20, vii. 16—17, 24—28, viii. 1—4, ix. 11—14, x. 19—23, xii. 22—24.

[2] Westcott *St. John's Epistles*, p. 36.

[3] 1 John ii. 1—2, Rev. v. 6.

Melchizedek, in the "blood of sprinkling," the "blood of an eternal covenant."

For the perversion of his ideas, in order to make the moment of death the chief moment of sacrifice, mediæval and Protestant theology are equally responsible. In part it was due to the misunderstanding of the idea of the priesthood after the order of Melchizedek. Melchizedek, said St. Cyprian and St. Clement, followed by the majority of the fathers,[1] offered bread and wine. That was the substance of his priestly sacrifice. It was therefore when Christ offered bread and wine at the Last Supper that He became a priest after the order of Melchizedek. In spite of this idea, however, the fathers—because the scriptural language is so constantly their pattern— clearly see that the priestly action of Christ is now in heaven, and that the earthly eucharists are to be viewed simply on the background of Christ's heavenly action.[2] But from the mediævalists this scriptural

[1] See Westcott *Hebrews*, pp. 200 ff.
[2] App. note 17, p. 308.

background fell away out of sight. At the Council of Trent therefore Christ was supposed to exercise His priesthood according to the order of Melchizedek through offering first in His own person at the Last Supper, and subsequently by His earthly ministers, bread and wine on earthly altars, *i.e.*, bread and wine transubstantiated into His body and blood. And there is no suggestion of any exercise of His priesthood in heaven at all. "Because His priesthood was not to be extinguished by His death," runs the Tridentine decree, "in the Last Supper, on the night in which He was betrayed—that He might leave to His own beloved spouse, the church, a visible sacrifice, such as the nature of man requires, whereby that blessed sacrifice once to be accomplished on the cross might be represented, and the memory of it remain, even unto the end of the world, and its salutary virtue be applied to the remission of those sins which we daily commit—declaring Himself constituted a priest for ever according to the order of Melchizedek, He offered up to God

THE TEST OF SCRIPTURE. 257

the Father His own body and blood under the species of bread and wine; and under the symbols of those same things He delivered His own body and blood to be received by His apostles, whom He then constituted the priests of the New Testament: and by the words 'Do this in remembrance of Me' He commanded them and their successors to offer, even as the catholic church has always understood and taught."[1] Here, as I say, the heavenly priesthood has passed out of the field of conception altogether.

But in the Epistle to the Hebrews the supposed offering by Melchizedek of bread and wine as elements of sacrifice, which at least it must be admitted does not appear distinctly in the narrative in Genesis,[2] is wholly ignored. The sole points in the narrative which are seized upon for comparison with Christ, are the union of kingship and priesthood in one person: the eternal life, which is symbolized in the abrupt manner of his appearance in history: and

[1] Decrees of Trent, *Sess.* xxii., cap. i.   [2] Gen. xiv. 18.

his superiority to the Levitical priesthood as contained in Abraham — the first two points being suggested in the 110th Psalm. The Protestants, however, when they rejected the Tridentine doctrine of the Melchizedekian priesthood, failed for the most part to fall back upon the plain ideas of the epistle. They still were bent upon finding the culminating moment of sacrifice on earth—that is, upon the cross of Calvary. Now viewed morally, in a case of *self*-sacrifice in which priest and sacrifice are necessarily one, the climax of sacrifice does occur at the point where the moral effort culminates—in the passion and on the cross. And it is so represented in the New Testament generally. But the New Testament as a whole refuses to allow us to separate the death from the life to which it leads up. Even in St. Paul it is Christ alive out of death who " reconciles us to God in one body," and " through whom we have access unto the Father in one Spirit," and " who maketh intercession for us " at the right hand of God.[1] More obviously this is

---

[1] Eph. ii. 16, 18; Rom. viii. 34.

THE TEST OF SCRIPTURE. 259

so in St. John. And in the special treatment of our atonement with God in the Epistle to the Hebrews, which to a great extent formed the basis for the eucharistic worship of the church, this is most abundantly true. Here the death is, for the most part, only regarded as the preparation of the priest and of His sacrifice, that He may enter into the true holy of holies in eternal effectiveness.

(b) Further, in the Epistle to the Hebrews, we Christians belong to, nay we constitute, the temple or house of God in which Christ offers Himself.[1] The veil which shrouds the most holy place is at least rent and laid open.[2] We have freedom of speech; boldness of approach;[3] and that because we are "partakers of the Christ" and "partakers of the Spirit,"[4] having been qualified for approaching the Most Holy by the "washing of water" and the "sprinkling of the blood."[5] Therefore we are admitted to all "the heavenly things" of the courts above: "we

[1] Hebr. iii. 6.
[2] vi. 19—20, ix. 8, x. 20.
[3] iii. 6, iv. 16, x. 19.
[4] iii. 14, vi. 4.
[5] x. 22.

are come unto ... Jesus the mediator and the blood of sprinkling."[1] We can make our spiritual sacrifices "through Christ."[2] All this affords the most natural atmosphere for eucharistic doctrine; and when therefore the author, incidentally and by implication, alludes to the privilege which all the children of the new covenant have, by distinction from even the priests of the old, namely that they can eat of their great offering for sin—" We have an altar, whereof they have no right to eat which serve the tabernacle,"[3] but we, it is implied, have—it cannot reasonably be disputed that he is referring to the familiar but solemn rite of the Holy Communion in which the Christians ate of the body and blood of their atoning sacrifice. The "altar" must mean the place where atonement is made, and this, according to the idea of this writer, is rather in the heavenly place than on the cross. According to the local imagery which he employs,

[1] Hebr. xii. 22—4.   [2] xiii. 15.
[3] xiii. 10. It is in this connection that the writer speaks of a "sacrifice of praise," and of beneficence, vv. 15—16.

it is something in heaven corresponding to the "golden altar" which belonged to the Jewish holy of holies.[1] But in a secondary sense it must mean the actual "table of the Lord" at which the Christians were fed with the sacrificial food, and which gained all its significance from being the earthly image of the reality in the heavens.

Thus, by the help of this epistle, we are brought back again to the central idea of the eucharist. It is a feast upon a sacrifice: but the feast upon the sacrifice is the culmination of the sacrifice. A sacrifice of which the worshippers may not eat can only be regarded as one in which the worshippers are admitted to imperfect fellowship with the God. To partake of the sacrifice is the way to have the most real share in its merit or efficacy. Therefore simply because the eucharist is a feeding upon the flesh and blood of our heavenly

[1] Hebr. ix. 4 (see the notes of Westcott and Davidson). For the altar in heaven see Rev. viii. 3. The fathers speak both of the altar in heaven (see pp. 84, 186, 189), and also more rarely of the cross as an altar, see Westcott *Hebrews*, p. 438, Johnson *Unbloody Sacr.* i. p. 80.

sacrifice, it is the occasion when we have the special right to bring all our offerings to be united to Him and offered by Him within the veil.

The same idea is suggested by St. Paul.[1] To "eat of a sacrifice" is, among Jews and Gentiles alike, to "have communion with the altar," and with the object of worship at the altar, the being to whom the sacrifice is offered. This set of ideas St. Paul applies to "the Lord's table" of the Christian church, as well as to the Jewish altars (whence the phrase, "the Lord's table," is derived)[2] and to the sacrificial banquets of the heathen. To St. Paul then, as to the author of the Epistle to the Hebrews, our eucharistic feeding on Christ implies a perfect fellowship in His sacrifice.

But this implication of the language of the apostolic writers carries us back to the words of Christ's institution.[3] These words

---

[1] 1 Cor. x. 18—22.

[2] Ezek. xliv. 16; Mal. i. 7, 12; Is. lxv. 11, R. V.

[3] On the critical and textual questions involved see app. note 18, p. 310.

give a rich depth of meaning to St. Paul's assertion that what is "proclaimed" at the eucharistic meal is the sacrificial death of the Lord.[1] For at the Last Supper our Lord solemnly blessed and broke and distributed to His disciples a certain loaf or portion of bread, and blessed and gave to them a certain cup of wine, and He declared that this bread and this cup were to be identified by the faith of His disciples with His body and His blood. Where their bodily eyes saw these outward symbols, with spiritual eyes they were to see the body and the blood; while with the mouth of the body they were to eat and drink the earthly food, with the mouth of faith they were to eat and drink the spiritual realities. But how were this body and blood characterized? Was it as " the body given *to* them," and " the blood given *to* them ? " No, it was as " the body which is [given] on their behalf"—the body,

[1] 1 Cor. xi. 26. Dr. Edersheim, *The Temple* (Rel. Tract Soc.) p. 199, remarks: "The very term for the Paschal liturgy itself, the *haggadah*, which means 'showing forth' (*cf.* Exod. xiii. 8), is exactly the same as that used by St. Paul in describing the service of the Lord's Supper."

that is, as given in sacrifice for them. And it was "the blood which is being poured out for many with a view to the remission of sins," that is the blood as sacrificially offered. The spiritual objects, therefore, which faith is to "discern" in the eucharist are not merely our spiritual food. They are that because first of all they are something else—our eternal and perfect sacrifice. That it is which is spiritually present in the midst of the worshipping church.

This appears more clearly as we examine our Lord's words with more exactness. "This is my body which is" (or "is being given") "on your behalf." Our Lord was then and there already at the Last Supper offering His body as a sacrifice for the salvation of mankind in will and intention.[1] He was going to offer it next day in the horrible reality of death. Raised and glorified, it was to be for ever the body of our eternal priest and sacrifice in the heavenly places. But, without special reference to those

[1] On the Last Supper in its relation to future eucharists see app. note 19, p. 312.

different moments of offering, it is certainly the body as being made a sacrifice on our behalf which is presented to our faith, and for our partaking, in the eucharist. We turn to the words spoken over the cup. At the inauguration of the old covenant, victims had been sacrificed, and half of their blood Moses had sprinkled on the altar, and the rest he "sprinkled" on the people, and said "Behold the blood of the covenant which the Lord hath made with you." So now at the inauguration of the new covenant our Lord says, "This is my blood which is being poured out with a view to the forgiveness of the world's sins." It is the blood of our propitiation which He was already offering in will and intention; which He was to shed next day upon the cross in physical fact; and in the power of which— the power of life surrendered and thereby made efficacious—He was to enter for ever into the heavenly place.

The word which is rendered "shed" in our versions should probably be rendered (as above) "poured out." It has in fact in the Greek of the Old Testament both meanings. It is used abundantly of blood as shed in slaughter, as in the phrase "their blood have they shed like water on every side of Jerusalem:"[1] but it is also used of the blood of victims as "poured out" at the altar,[2] that is, of blood as having passed through death and become available as an instrument of propitiation. No doubt, in the case of our Lord, the unity of moral will through every stage of the sacrificial action takes the edge off the clearness of the distinction. In shedding His blood He was also offering it. Still the precise force of the word[3] is, in all probability, "This is My blood, *which is being sacrificially poured out*," which again is equivalent to " This is the blood of sprinkling of the new covenant" —the blood of sacrificial efficacy.

[1] Ps. lxxix. 3, and in about forty other places.

[2] Exod. xxix. 12; Lev. iv. 7, 18, 25, 30, 34, viii. 15, ix. 9; 2 K. xvi. 15. Dr. Edersheim remarks how the blood of the Paschal lambs was poured out—"jerked in one jet at the base of the altar" (*l.c.* p. 191).

[3] As in the case of the similar words αἱματεκχυσία and πρόσχυσις in Hebr. ix. 22, xi. 28.

Here, then, we have the profoundest justification for the doctrine of the eucharistic sacrifice, especially as it is held and taught in the East, and, at least of recent years, among ourselves. What, according to this teaching, especially constitutes the eucharistic sacrifice is the fact that the eternal sacrifice is made present to faith in the midst of the worshipping church. "Ye are come unto Jesus the mediator and to the blood of sprinkling." Granted this, all the lower earthly sacrifices of prayers, alms, oblations and commemorations group themselves naturally and inevitably round this central moment. All that is necessary to keep this doctrine in full touch with the institution of Christ is the frank recognition that the bond of union or point of connection with Christ our sacrifice lies in communion, and nowhere short of this, except in a very secondary and inferior sense: and that this applies to the Christian people as much as to the priest who is the minister of the eucharistic liturgy.

It is possible that other words of Christ

at the institution of the eucharist yield the sacrificial meaning with at least as great directness: that the word translated "do" ("This do in remembrance of me") really means "offer," and "remembrance" really means "commemoration before God": but on these points the evidence is conflicting, and does not warrant assertion.[1] But certainly the argument securely derived from the language of Christ, as explained above, is strengthened when we consider that the background of His new institution was the chief annual sacrificial meal of the old covenant. It was by feasting on the paschal victim that the Israelite annually renewed his fellowship in the covenant of the ancient people; and similarly the object of feasting upon the true paschal victim is to renew our fellowship in the covenant which is inaugurated in His blood—the covenant of free and unhindered approach to the Father.

[1] On the sacrificial meaning of ποιεῖν and ἀνάμνησις see app. note 20, p. 312.

CHAPTER V.

OUR PRESENT SERVICE OF HOLY COMMUNION.

IF the contentions of the previous chapters are in any measure sound, the eucharistic doctrine which they have been intended to express corresponds accurately with what our portion of the church catholic lays it upon her clergy to teach—that is to say, it is "agreeable to the doctrine of the Old and New Testaments, and it is what the catholic fathers and ancient bishops have collected out of the said doctrine." It remains for us, therefore, to return upon our present liturgy and seek to form an estimate of it in the light of the principles to which it appeals; but now only so far as concerns what one may call its secondary doctrinal features. For with ceremonial questions we are not in these chapters concerned, except as they represent doctrine:

and on the position of our present Prayer Book with regard to the main aspects of eucharistic doctrine enough has already been said. But its subordinate doctrinal features are specially characteristic.[1]

It represents a reformation of the mediæval liturgy and practice of the church in England on the basis of certain principles: especially its object was (1) to make the worship "common" to priest and people; and (2) to restore the communion of the people to its original prominence.

(1) The community of worship between priest and people was emphasized chiefly by the translation of the service into the vernacular; by the abolition of stated prayers to be said secretly by the priest, which means that all the appointed service is to be "rehearsed distinctly"; and by the requirement that the great central action of "the breaking of the bread" is to be performed "before the people."

[1] For a most thorough and comprehensive review of the Prayer Book liturgy, I very thankfully refer to the new edition of Procter's *Book of Common Prayer*, by W. H. Frere (Macmillan, 1901), pp. 430 ff.

It cannot be doubted that these changes and requirements are justifiable and represent the original principle of catholic worship. For that principle certainly was that the ministerial priest is but the divinely appointed and empowered organ of the whole priestly body, and that the offering belongs to the body as a whole and is its common act. For example the secret saying of the *anaphora*, or specially of the prayer of consecration, which began to gain ground in the sixth century and which Justinian sought to check as an abuse,[1] is quite out of harmony with the language of St. Paul and of the liturgies, which certainly makes the breaking and the blessing and the offering the acts of the whole body, though the celebrating minister is both the voice which blesses and the hand which breaks and offers.[2] In the great Amen which from apostolic times has closed the eucharistic prayer the people are to identify themselves with the action and words of the minister

---

[1] See Brightman, p. 533, n.4. [2] See above, p. 213.

in which throughout they have been taking intelligent part.[1]

The concealing of the altar and the central eucharistic action by a veil was a practice which went back at least to the fourth century, and was intended to express —not any isolation of the priest from the people—but the truth that "the mysteries" were heavenly things, and that the veil which hid the true holy of holies, though it had been rent, had not been removed. The voice of the unseen celebrant sounded as Christ's voice in heaven, and when he came out to administer the gifts he came as "in the person of Christ" out of heaven.[2] Moreover the removal of the front portion of the veil in the middle ages in the West —leaving the altar only with wings, or veils at the side—was due to a desire that the people should see the elevation of the

[1] 1 Cor. xiv. 16.

[2] See Bingham *Antiq.* VIII. vi. 8. This "mystical veil" is under various names mentioned by Athanasius, Synesius, and Chrysostom, who also indicates its meaning.

OUR PRESENT COMMUNION SERVICE. 273

host.[1] It was thus one result of what must be called the lowering of theological conception by which the eucharist was brought down from heaven to earth.

Our present liturgy however will have neither the suppression of the priest's voice, nor any veiling of his action, nor any concealment of the meaning of the service in a dead language. In this respect it has returned to what was doubtless the original method of Christian worship; the method which expresses as simply as possible the idea of a common worship "in spirit and in truth." The idea and method then are good and sound. All that we have to deplore is that the idea is so inadequately realized amongst us: that corporate eucharistic worship is so little understood.

(2) In restoring to its proper prominence the communion of the people and their communion in both kinds, those who fixed our present service were still aiming at the same end of making the whole action, up to its

[1] A practice which began with the thirteenth century in England.

culminating point in communion, common to priest and people according to their several functions. And here there is no room at all for doubt that they were true to the real intention of the eucharist and the proper mind of the church. This has already been made abundantly plain.

So strongly was this intention enforced that the directions of our Prayer Book were deliberately calculated to make the communion of the people, or of a sufficient number of their representatives, an indispensable element in a celebration of the eucharist; so much so that, when communicants were not forthcoming, the celebration was not to take place.

The result of this was that, unaccustomed as the people had become before the Reformation to anything more than very infrequent communions,[1] they were not to be prevailed upon very largely to alter their practice: and the great Christian service—the only

[1] The demand of the Devonshire rebels (1549) was to "have the sacrament of the altar but at Easter delivered to the lay people."

service of our Lord's special institution—became, after an ineffectual struggle to secure the celebration each Sunday,[1] an occasional affair; a sort of occasional appendage to the Sunday worship instead of its manifest and central act. Certainly nothing could have been more contrary to ancient catholic custom and principle than this.

We have to be thankful that recovery has now reached to a point at which it may be said that in very few places is it difficult to secure a sufficient number of faithful communicants to make possible the Sunday eucharist. As to week-day eucharists, or the continual daily eucharist, the habits of the church catholic have presented such varieties that one part of the church is thoroughly justified in making the frequency of celebration normally dependent upon the presence of a certain number of persons desiring to communicate. There is nothing in principles that can be called catholic which justifies us in rebelling against such a prescription.

[1] See Frere *l.c.* pp. 498 f.

It still remains for us however to restore the eucharist to its central place as the chief, if not the most largely attended,[1] act of Sunday worship. With nothing short of this may we be content. But also we must not be content with restoring as our chief act of worship a eucharist at which the communion of the people does not form an important part. It cannot be said too strongly that any practice which divorces eucharistic worship and sacrifice from communion, or which rests content at the "high service" with the communion of the priest alone, really represents a seriously defective theology.

No doubt with our modern habits of late rising on Sunday it is extremely difficult to make the common parochial communion appear in any sense as the chief act of

---

[1] For it cannot be said that catholic principle justifies our encouraging those who are not occasional communicants, nor preparing to become so, to be present at the eucharist. The right point in the service for such people to withdraw is surely after the sermon, but before the presentation of the oblations. This the structure of the ancient liturgies suggests, and such was the English custom until recently.

worship, without an undue disregard of the very ancient and venerable tradition of communicating fasting. But the fact is that hitherto the difficulty has not been seriously faced by any considerable body of people who are prepared equally to insist upon all the elements necessary to a right solution.

There is in our present service book no direction for those to withdraw who are not at the moment intending to communicate; and they have a perfect right to exercise the liberty to remain without communicating, which, as appears elsewhere, was commonly exercised by the faithful as early as the end of the second century.[1] We may well feel that to "assist in the prayers" is better than to be absent. But the principles of eucharistic worship which run deepest into the theology of the incarnation and of the Holy Spirit will never allow us to raise such attendance without communion to a very much higher level of principle than attendance at other kinds of corporate worship. It is a matter which must be looked at

[1] See quotation from Clement, pp. 307—8.

impartially from the point of view of education in worship.

Among other principles which our present service emphasizes we may notice—

(3) The combination in one act of worship of preaching the word with celebrating the sacrament. This principle was expressed in the exhortations which are so abundantly supplied, as well as in the provision for a sermon or homily at every celebration. We have somewhat wearied of this perhaps more than abundant provision. But it cannot be doubted that the principle of coupling the food of the divine word with that of the grace of sacraments is justified by appeal to our Lord's institution, to apostolic practice, and to the ancient traditions of eucharistic worship.[1]

(4) The restoration of communion in both kinds. With regard to the importance of this it would be hard to use too strong language. And, in restoring to the laity the communion in the blood of Christ, the idea was again brought forward in the

[1] See also pp. 8, 291.

"prayer of humble access" that a distinct kind of spiritual effect is to be attributed to the gift of the body and of the blood of our Lord—a cleansing of our sinful bodies by His body, and a washing of our souls by His blood :[1] and in each case a spiritual effect intended for all alike.

The mediæval doctrine that "the whole Christ is present in each particle of either kind"[2] can hardly be *denied* by any one who affirms the indivisible spiritual unity of the living Christ; but in view of our Lord's

[1] This idea of the distinction is not original: *cf.* in the ancient and well-known prayers ascribed to St. Ambrose or St. Anselm, "We are washed [by the blood] and sanctified [by the body]": and also Raymund of Sabunde *l.c.* tit. 287, "The bread signifies the body and the wine signifies the soul (or 'life'—*anima*); because bread appertains to flesh and wine to blood, in which is the seat of the soul (or 'life')." The idea admitted of being abused, as if the body of Christ was directly for our body only, and the blood only for our souls: see Frere *l.c.* p. 494. This is guarded against by the language of the catechism, which declares that as our bodies are strengthened by both bread and wine, so are our souls by both the body and the blood —our souls directly, and our bodies only indirectly through the renewal of our spirits.

[2] First found in Hildebert and Anselm; see *Dissert.* p. 266.

institution of the communion in two kinds, it is indeed wonderful how Christians can prefer to trust a very fallible logic of sacramental presence rather than the manifested intention of our Lord.

With regard to the details of our service a very few points call for notice here—and those only in the central part of the service, where alone questions of eucharistic doctrine are suggested.

The position assigned in our service to the intercession—at the beginning of the eucharistic portion proper, and as an accompaniment to the presentation of the elements on the altar and the offering of the alms and oblations[1] of the people—was, in fact, whether the reformers knew it or not, a return to the original practice of the church in general and the Gallican rite in particular.

But the omission of any clear prayer for

---

[1] The "oblations" meant strictly the offerings made for the support of the clergy; see Frere *l.c.* p. 482, and reff. But the word was interpreted almost from the time of its insertion, and probably in accordance with the intention of some of those responsible for it, of the bread and wine, in accordance with primitive language.

the departed is a grievous departure from primitive and universal practice : a grievous instance of ill-regulated reaction, for the reversal of which, with all proper safeguards, we may now hopefully pray.

No doubt it must also be admitted that the whole of our *anaphora* represents a wide departure from the primitive type.

The solemn appeal of the *Sursum corda*, leading on to the great thanksgiving for the revelation of God in creation and redemption, which included the angelic hymn of adoration addressed to the Thrice-Holy; and then the recital before the Father of the words of our Lord in instituting the eucharist before His passion, leading on, in obedience to the command to do this in remembrance of Him, to the solemn commemoration by the church of His passion, death, resurrection, and ascension, and the expected second coming; and the offering of the representative gifts of bread and wine, and the invocation of the Holy Spirit, or of the divine power, to consecrate them to be the body and blood of Christ for the reception of the faithful;

then, whether preceded or no by renewed intercessions for the living and the dead, the recitation of the Our Father as the prayer proper to accepted sons; and lastly, after a prayer of preparation, the breaking of the bread, and the communion all together in the holy gifts—this unbroken order of ancient eucharistic worship seems to express all the truth which, in this connection, the church knows how to express, and to leave nothing out. Any omission or alteration appears to be for the worse.

It had never been so strikingly or richly represented in the Latin as in the Greek service. All its elements however had been represented in the West, and continued to be so adequately enough in our service of 1549; but the subsequent alterations have certainly made our service singularly unprimitive in structure and by no means suggestive of those deeper doctrines which are the best correction of mediæval errors.

For the service of the mass simply translated would not have suggested these errors —neither transubstantiation nor the renewal of the sacrifice of Calvary. The canon is indeed actually impatient of the interpretation which the theology of transubstantiation requires. For after that the words of institution, which are believed to be the specific instruments of transubstantiation, have been recited, the canon still speaks of the elements as offerings of an earthly sort like the offerings of Abraham and Melchizedek: and by its commemoration of the resurrection and ascension of our Lord, and its subsequent mention of the heavenly altar, it afforded an admirable opportunity for a return to the ancient way of thinking of the mingling of earthly and heavenly things, and the ancient idea of fellowship with the heavenly Christ.

But our present service has split up the order of the continuous eucharistic action by transposing the "prayer of humble access" from its earlier and natural place before communion to its present place between the *Sanctus* and the prayer of consecration; and, what is of greater importance, also by interposing the communion between the consecration and the Lord's Prayer with the prayer of oblation. But, what is most to be lamented, it has suppressed all commemoration and mention of the resurrection and ascension and the heavenly ministry and the Holy Ghost. The whole action, as far as words can do it, is brought down to earth as in no other liturgy. The mediæval western idea that the words of institution constitute alone the form of consecration is stereotyped as in no other liturgy by the abrupt termination of the prayer of consecration as soon as they are recited, and by the directions given for additional consecration with the bare use of these words, when more of the consecrated gifts are needed for distribution.

As for our present prayer of oblation, if we had been preserved from the grave mistakes which have just been deplored, it might in its present position have admitted of something more than justification. For in itself it expresses admirably and richly the doctrine of which St. Augustine is the special exponent—the doctrine that the culmination of sacrifice is in the oblation of the faithful, made more deeply than before members of the body by their communion in the Lord's body, and thus becoming themselves the sacrifice which, in Christ, is offered to the Father. And the prayer directly following (which surely should be additional and not alternative), the prayer of thanksgiving for communion, is again Augustinian in the emphasis that it lays upon membership in the church as the gift of communion.

Of course, we must remember that there was strong pressure upon the Reformers to make even more trenchant and disastrous alterations than in fact were made: and that the movement since Elizabeth's accession has been continually one of recovery, which, as far as the eucharist is concerned, has taken fuller effect in Scotland and America than in England itself. We must be thankful indeed for the restraining and restoring hand of God. But we must not suffer ourselves to forget that the appeal to antiquity is not, either in our doctrinal statements about the eucharist or in our rite for celebrating it, adequately carried out. It is an appeal which leaves us still much to do. And what there is still to be done, as has appeared already, will put a strain on both of the parties and tendencies which have always, since the Reformation, existed among us, and not on one only. It will lay upon all alike the duty of learning old truths anew.

Finally, if there is one element of eucharistic doctrine more than another which we need to strive to restore, it is what our prayer of thanksgiving after communion so nobly expresses, the idea that fellowship in Christ is fellowship in the church—that by receiving His body from above, we are to become His body on earth. A miserable individualism in our thoughts of holy communion has taken the place of the rich and moving thought which in ancient days was so prominent, that through fellowship in the perfect sacrifice of the Son of Man, we ourselves become that sacrifice. That is to say, we can only plead His passion if we are prepared to enter into unity of spirit and life with Him who offered and presents it. And the unity of spirit and life means a sacrificial manner of living. And the way in which the sacrificial manner of living is to show itself is in real brotherliness: it is in those habitual and considerate good works of love by which the body of Christ on earth is to be bound together. It is by mutual kindness and sociability, real and equal consideration, large forbearance and toleration of differences of disposition and taste and opinion; by a vivid belief that if one member suffer all the members suffer with it; and by true regard for the whole interests of each other, in body as well as spirit, in respect of outward conditions as well as those that are inward. It is by a love which, as St. Augustine says, recognizes no limit, but grows till it is as large as the world, and which hates nothing so much as schism in the body, or division of any kind between man and man: but which manifests itself primarily not by any action of the church on the world without, but by the love she shows within her own wide and catholic membership, because the common Spirit who dwells within makes a fellowship possible which, apart from this union with God, could not be. " By this shall all men know that ye are my disciples, if ye have love one to another." " We know that we have passed from death unto life because we love the brethren."[1]

It does not indeed need saying that, if St. Augustine is right in making the doctrine of brotherhood the ultimate goal of eucharistic teaching, there is a great deal for us to do and teach : and that what we have to do and teach is exactly what both coincides with the best tendency of our times towards the ideas of divine fatherhood and human brotherhood, and is also best calculated to correct its inherent weaknesses.

For the weaknesses inherent in mere philanthropy and in the current conceptions of brotherhood require for their correction exactly that of which the eucharist is the very instrument and perpetual renewal—the life of fellowship and intercourse with God in Christ, the life which is "hid with Christ in God," and which draws its strength and its inspiration from the divine sacrifice perpetually renewed within.

[1] See further app. note 21, p. 316.

APPENDED NOTES.

NOTE I, see p. 7.

Justin Martyr on the eucharistic "word of prayer."

WHAT exactly Justin Martyr means by the "prayer-word which is from Christ," by which the eucharist is blessed, is, and will probably remain, uncertain. Any form of benediction of the elements believed by the church to be substantially what Christ used, or any form of prayer repeating His words of institution, would answer sufficiently to Justin's description. The suggestion that Justin means the Lord's Prayer is surely improbable. The Lord's Prayer is not a form of thanksgiving or benediction over food.

No doubt Gregory the Great (*Epp.* ix. 12, *P. L.* lxxvii. 957) gives it as the reason why he had introduced the Lord's Prayer into the Roman canon immediately after the consecration, "that the custom of the apostles was to consecrate the sacrifice of the oblation with this prayer only—*ad ipsam solummodo orationem.*" But Gregory's authority is hardly adequate to substantiate his assertion, or to interpret Justin. Justin must mean by his "word of prayer" what Irenæus calls a "word of God" (see *C. haer.* v. 2. 2—3). "The cup which is from nature He confessed to be His own blood, from which He invigorates our blood; and the bread which is from nature He asserted to be His own body, from which He makes our bodies grow. Since therefore both the mingled cup, and the bread which has been made, receives upon itself *the word of God* and becomes the eucharist of the blood and body of Christ (or 'the eucharist becomes the body of Christ') and the substance of our flesh grows and consists of these, etc." The same circle of ideas and phrases is common to Justin and Irenæus. And "a word of God" must mean some formula of benediction and not the Lord's Prayer. Irenæus repeats the phrase just below the passage quoted.

NOTE 2, see p. 22.

Eating Christ's flesh explained to mean receiving His teaching.

This proposed explanation is based on a misunderstanding (as I am persuaded it is) of St. John vi. 63: "The flesh profiteth nothing: the words that I have spoken unto you are spirit and are life." Some, in early as well as later times (see *Dissertations*, pp. 303 ff.), have interpreted these words: "By My life-giving flesh and blood I did not really mean flesh at all, for it could do you no good: I meant My spiritual, life-giving teaching." But this

APPENDED NOTES.

explanation renders our Lord's strong insistence upon the figure—one may venture to say the misleading figure—of flesh and blood quite unintelligible. It is more in accordance with the whole context and the Greek words to understand " The flesh profiteth nothing" as equivalent to "*mere* flesh —flesh of itself—profiteth nothing." Then the whole verse will mean, "*Mere flesh*, as you naturally think of it, *profits nothing*. But the things I have just spoken to you of—the flesh and blood of the glorified Son of Man (ver. 62)—are something much more than mere flesh and blood; they *are spirit and (therefore) life*." See *Dissert*. p. 305, and *cf*. Lk. ii. 15—17, where " word" (ῥῆμα) is used both for the word as uttered and for the thing spoken about. This is a Hebraism. See also John iii. 11, " We speak (λαλοῦμεν, *i.e.*, speak about) that we do know."

Of course it remains true that the words of God are spiritual food and a real nourishment of the intelligence, as " the flesh and blood of Christ" are of the whole manhood: *cf*. Jer. xv. 16, Ezek. iii. 1—3, Ps. xix. 10, Rev. x. 9. Indeed it is a matter which needs very careful consideration, that the sacramental feeding cannot profitably continue without the " reading, marking, learning and inwardly digesting" of the words of God. Unless our intelligence is continually being spiritually nourished and enlightened, our whole nature is starved and withered, and the sacramental nourishment is comparatively ineffectual.

NOTE 3, see p. 44.

The ritual of the Roman church.

On this subject we should consult Duchesne *l.c.* pp. 165, 175 ff., and *Liber Pontificalis* i. 169, on the *fermentum*. Also a most interesting paper by Mr. Edmund Bishop on *The Genius of the Roman Rite* (Beaufort House Printing Works). He points out the extreme simplicity of the pure Roman rite until it was largely interpolated with elements from Gallican sources. The *Gloria in Excelsis*, the Creed, the censing of the altar, the elevation, adorations, etc., the *Agnus Dei* (probably), with other prayers and chants, are such interpolations. The element of ritual pomp was concentrated in the original rite upon the two moments: (1) the first solemn entry of the celebrant and his ministers, especially on great feasts, with torches, incense, etc., and (2) the preparation for the reading of the Gospel. The two points in the rite which are most elaborately described in the early Roman *ordines* are the collection of the oblations of bread and wine from the people, and the "fraction" of the bread preparatory to the communion, *i.e.*, the two points at which the *corporate* aspect of the service is most conspicuous.

NOTE 4, see p. 58.

Ignatius of Antioch on the eucharist.

The passages quoted already in the text are from *ad Smyrn.* 7, *ad Philad.* 4, *ad Eph.* 20. There can, I think, be no legitimate dispute as to the realism of Ignatius' belief in the eucharist. No doubt he sometimes used expressions which are hard exactly to define: as "faith which is the flesh of the Lord, and love which is the blood of Jesus Christ" (*Trall.* 8); "the bread of God which is the flesh of Jesus Christ and His blood which is incorruptible love" (*Rom.* 7); "the blood of Christ which is eternal and abiding joy" (*Philad.* tit.). But these expressions are probably intended to describe vividly the moral quality or substance of the life of union with Christ. And on the whole one cannot but feel that Ignatius of all men was most penetrated with the sense of a union of Christ with His church "*both in the flesh and in the spirit.*" See *Eph.* 10, *Magn.* 13, *Smyrn.* 12.

NOTE 5, see p. 75.

The reverent care of the sacred elements in the early ages.

The evidence from Alexandria is supplied by Origen *in Exod. hom.* xiii. 3. He is exhorting his hearers to be as reverent in receiving the word of God in sermons as in receiving the sacramental body. "You know, you who are accustomed to assist at the holy mysteries, how, when you receive the Lord's body, you hold it with all caution and veneration, lest any fragment of it should fall, or any portion of the consecrated gift be lost. For you think yourselves guilty, and you justly think so, if any of it through negligence be allowed to fall. But if you use such caution, and rightly, in holding His body, why do you think it is less impiety to treat with contumely the word of God?" For Africa, see Tertullian's precisely similar language, *de cor. mil.* 3. For Jerusalem, see Cyril, *catech.* xxiii. 21. For Rome, (?) c. 200 (probably), see *Canones Hippolyti* xxix. 209—with the superstitious reason "ne potiatur eo spiritus malignus," instead of the ethical motive of reverence. Dom Morin has recently (*Revue Benedictine*, July, 1900, pp. 243 ff.) argued that the so-called Canons of Hippolytus are really the "ministerial letter" mentioned by Eusebius as sent to Rome by Dionysius of Alexandria (c. 260) through a certain Hippolytus. In that case they would not supply evidence of Roman customs. But, in any case, the African custom would presumably be derived from Rome.

NOTE 6, see p. 76.

The language used by some of the Fathers as to a change in the water in baptism and in the chrism, similar to the change in the eucharistic elements.

Waterland (*op. cit.* p. 159) and many others have made use of this language to prove that the fathers did not really believe in any objective presence in the eucharistic elements any more than in the water of baptism or the chrism. But the language referred to is admirably discussed by

Dr. Gifford (see above, p. 57, n.²). He shows that the "change" described by Cyril of Jerusalem, who is chiefly relied upon in this connection, is a change of use only. "The water acquires a power of sanctity," later described as "the grace given by the water" (*Cat.* iii. 3, 4): "the ointment becomes a gift of Christ and effectual to impart, by the presence of the Holy Ghost, His divine nature" (xxi. 3). But neither the water nor the chrism are said to become something which exists by itself, as the bread is said to "become the body of Christ," and the wine to "become the blood of Christ," to be treated with religious worship (as Cyril would have the eucharistic elements to be, see p. 104) as in some sense identical with those heavenly substances.

NOTE 7, see p. 82.
Irenæus on the invocation.

In the first of the passages referred to above ἔκκλησιν (evocation), not ἐπίκλησιν (invocation), has been commonly supposed to be the reading of the Greek fragment cited by John of Damascus. But Harnack has recently discovered that this is a mistake of the printed texts—the MSS. read ἐπίκλησιν; see *Texte u. Untersuch.*, Neue Folge, v. 3, p. 56. This discovery is one point in his overwhelming indictment of the Lutheran Pfaff of having forged the fragments of Irenæus which he professed to discover. Certainly they must no longer be quoted as words of Irenæus.

NOTE 8, see p. 95.

Victorinus Afer on an objective presence of Christ in the eucharist.

In this connection I should like to refer to a phrase which Victorinus Afer quotes from the (presumably Roman) "prayer of the oblation" of his day (c. 360) both in Greek and Latin. See *adv. Ar.* ii. 8 (*P. L.* viii. 1094)—"Oratio oblationis intellectu eodem precatur Deum: σῶσον περιούσιον λαὸν ζηλωτὴν καλῶν ἔργων." But previously (*l.c.* i. 30, col. 1063): "Sicuti et in oblatione dicitur: Munda tibi populum circumvitalem aemulatorem bonorum operum *circa tuam substantiam venientem.*" And in this barbaric version of περιούσιον he interprets "substantia" of the substance, or life, of Jesus as given in the eucharist, which the Christian people are represented as "coming around."

This reference of Victorinus to the two languages probably implies that in his day both Greek and Latin were in use in the liturgy of the Roman church.

NOTE 9, see p. 130.

Later Westerns on the spirituality of the eucharistic presence.

Hildebert of Tours (12th century) *de sacr. altaris*, c. 2 (see *SS. Patr. Opusc. Sel.* xxxix. 276 f.): "The body of Christ is in one place only in a natural manner, but in many places in a virtual manner.

In one place by nature, in many by grace and divine virtue. In one in a corporal manner, in many in a spiritual manner. For it belongs not to a body, but to a spirit, to be in many places at once." The Decree of Trent (sess. xiii., c. 1) declares that Christ is "in heaven according to the natural mode of existence, and that nevertheless He is, in many other places, sacramentally present to us in His own substance by a manner of existing which, though we can scarcely express it in words, yet can we by the understanding illuminated by faith conceive, and we ought most firmly to believe to be possible with God." "If place," writes Cardinal Newman, "is excluded from the idea of the sacramental presence, therefore division or distance from heaven is excluded also. . . . Moreover, if the idea of distance is excluded, therefore is the idea of motion. Our Lord then neither descends from heaven upon our altars, nor moves when carried in procession. The visible species change their position but He does not move. He is in the Holy Eucharist after the manner of a spirit." (*Via Media*, ii. p. 220. ed. 1877.) A "corporal presence of Christ's natural flesh and blood," as it exists in heaven, is all that the *Declaration on Kneeling*, appended to our Communion Service, excludes. The Revisers of 1662 declined to exclude a "real and essential" presence. On the other hand, the Declaration gives a positive reason for kneeling which involves no objective presence at all. It leaves the question open. (See p. 232.)

NOTE 10, see p. 134.

Reservation of the sacrament, and the treatment of it after communion.

The carrying of portions of the sacrament to absent brethren from the common eucharist is mentioned by Justin Martyr (see above, p. 9). Tertullian also assures us that in Africa the Christians habitually carried the sacrament home to communicate themselves: see p. 307 and *ad uxor.* ii. 5. And the following letter of St. Basil (*ep.* 93), which is less familiar, is worth transcribing:—

"It is good and profitable to communicate every day and receive the holy body and blood of Christ; He Himself plainly saying, He that eateth My flesh and drinketh My blood hath eternal life. For who can dispute that continually to partake of the life is nothing else than abundantly to live? For ourselves, we communicate four times a week—Sunday, Wednesday, Friday and Saturday; and other days if they are saints'-days. But that in times of persecution, where there is no bishop or priest present, a man should be compelled to take the communion with his own hand—that this is no grievous matter it is superfluous to prove, for long custom confirms what we say by the evidence of facts.

"All those who live in solitude, as monks or hermits, where there is no priest, communicate themselves. And in Alexandria and Egypt each one of the lay people for the most part has the communion in his own house, and, when he will, communicates himself. For when once the priest has consecrated the sacrifice and delivered it, he who has once received it as a whole and partakes of it day by day ought to believe that he partakes and receives from the hand of him who first gave it. For even in the church the priest gives each man his portion, and he who receives it holds it with full control, and so carries it to his mouth with his own hand. It is then the same thing virtually, whether a man receives only one portion from the priest or several portions at once." Elsewhere St. Basil gives rules for reverence in private reception.

It appears to be certainly true that the reserved sacrament was not the object of outward worship in the ancient Church, as indeed, apart from the use of it to communicate the sick, it still is not in the orthodox East. This at least I believe, and to a small extent have observed, to be the case. And the portions of the consecrated elements that remained after communion were treated in a way that suggests an attitude towards them different from the modern. Thus it was an ancient custom at Constantinople in A.D. 590 (see Evagrius, *H. E.* iv. 36; *P. G.* lxxxvi. (2), 2770) which subsisted up to 1333 to give them to children fetched from the school. (In A.D. 588 a council at Mâcon strove to introduce the practice into France, but would have the children fasting.) At Jerusalem it was the custom to consume them with fire; see Scudamore *Notit. Euch.* (Longmans, 1892), pp. 782 ff.

But strange as these customs may appear they were not based upon disbelief in the permanence of the effect of consecration, for Evagrius tells us of the practice thus—" It is an ancient practice at Constantinople that as often as a great quantity of the sacred portions of the undefiled body of Christ our God be left over, unpolluted children be sent for from the school to eat them." And the reason of his telling us this is to record a miracle which occurred in the case of a Jewish child who had received among the rest. Moreover Cyril of Alexandria condemns those who in his day suggested "that the mystic gift is of no avail if a remnant of it be left till the morrow. For they who say this talk madly, for neither is Christ changed nor will His holy body be altered, but the virtue of the gift and His quickening grace are permanent in it." (*Ep. ad Calosir, P. G.* lxxvi. 1063 f.)

NOTE 11, see p. 172.

Irenæus on the sacrifice in the eucharist.

Irenæus quite certainly regards the eucharist as a sacrifice to God of the firstfruits of the ground, bread and wine, directed by prayer towards the heavenly altar, and consecrated to become the body and blood of Christ. Does he, like Cyril or Chrysostom, regard the presence of the body and blood not only as the occasion for communion, but also as the special occasion for pleading or presenting Christ as our sacrifice? One passage (iv. 18. 4) is alleged for an affirmative reply. " This oblation (of firstfruits) the Church alone offers pure to the Creator, offering to Him, with giving of thanks, what is of His own creation. But the Jews do not offer it; for their hands are full of blood: for they did not receive (or 'have not received') the word which is offered [to God]." The Greek does not remain. The Latin is: "non enim receperunt verbum [per] quod offertur [Deo]"—the words in brackets being uncertain. How are we to interpret the phrase?

The point of the passage is to speak of the outward offering as commended by the pure heart of the offerers. Irenæus goes on to speak of the bread and wine as being, in virtue of the thanksgiving (eucharist) made over it, the body and blood of the Lord who is the Son *and Word* of the Father, Himself the instrument of their creation. Later he speaks of *the Word* as having given orders to make sacrifices (iv. 18. 6). Elsewhere he speaks of the bread and wine as " receiving upon themselves *the word of God*," *i.e.* the prayer of invocation, and becoming eucharist, the body and blood of Christ (v. 2. 3). Thus, according to what reading we adopt, four interpretations of the phrase in question suggest themselves:—

1. [Omitting *per*] " They have not received the Word who is offered to God ": *i.e.*, the Christ who is present in His body and blood as the substance

of the sacrifice. But this is alien to Irenæus' language in general. He does not in fact anywhere speak of *Christ* as present in the elements (*cf.* above, p. 63). Nor could "the Word" be a natural expression for the incarnate Christ, as present in the eucharist. Moreover this interpretation does not harmonize with the context.

2. [Reading *per*] "They have not received the word (*i.e.*, the gospel message) through which the offering is made to God." This makes good sense, and is probably right, if this reading is justified.

3. [Still reading *per*] "They have not received the Word [Christ] through whom the offering is made to God"; *cf.* iv. xvii. 6: "in Deo omnipotente *per Jesum Christium* offert eclesia."

4. [Omitting *per* and *Deo*] "They have not received the Word coming to them" (*cf.* John i. 11) or "the message of God proffered to them." The Greek would have been τὸν προσφερόμενον λόγον, and may have been misunderstood by the translator: *cf.* Justin, *Apol.* i. 13, for two ambiguous uses of προσφέρειν in a sacrificial context.

NOTE 12, see p. 175.

Passages in the Fathers where the immolation of Christ appears to be spoken of as repeated.

It is obvious that the language of dramatic representation easily slides into that of real repetition. A good example of ambiguous language, the real meaning of which remains, nevertheless, sufficiently plain, is to be found in the following famous passage from St. Gregory the Great (*Dial.* iv. 58). "For this victim [the eucharistic sacrifice] in a unique manner saves the soul from eternal death. It in fact renews (*reparat*) for us in a mystery the death of the Only-Begotten, who, though rising from death He dieth no more and death shall have no more dominion over Him, yet, living in Himself immortally and incorruptibly, is immolated for us over and over again in the mystery of the holy oblation. For there His body is taken and His flesh is shared for the salvation of His people, and His blood is poured out—not now into the hands of unbelievers, but into the mouths of the faithful. In view of this therefore let us weigh the magnitude of the sacrifice for us, which for our deliverance continually imitates the passion of the only-begotten Son. For which of the faithful can doubt that at the very hour of immolation, at the voice of the priest, the heavens are opened; that in that mystery of Jesus Christ the choirs of angels are present, the things highest and lowest are associated, the things earthly united with things heavenly, and the things invisible and visible made one? 59. But it is necessary, when we enact (*agamus*) these things, that we should sacrifice (*mactemus*) ourselves in contrition of heart, because we who celebrate the mysteries of the Lord's passion ought to imitate what we enact. For then (only) will He truly be the victim for us to God, when we have made ourselves a victim."

NOTE 13, see p. 179.

Errors current in the later middle ages about the sacrifices of masses.

On this subject an important passage is in *de ss. euch. sacr., serm.* 1, printed with the works of Albertus Magnus (Lyons, 1651), tom. xii. p. 250: " The second cause of the institution of this sacrament is the sacrifice of the altar, against a certain daily ravage effected by our sins:—that as the body of the Lord was once offered on the cross for original guilt (*debitum*), so for our daily offences (*delictis*) it might be continually offered on the altar, and the church might have in this a gift to make God propitious to herself (*ad placandum sibi Deum*), precious and acceptable beyond all the sacraments and sacrifices of the Law." On the authorship of these sermons—which are not by Albertus—see Vacant, *Histoire de la conception du sacrifice de la messe* (Paris and Lyons, 1894), p. 41. The Confession of Augsburg, pt. ii. art. 3, says, " The opinion came in vogue (*accessit*) which gave an infinite increase to private masses—namely, that Christ by His passion satisfied for original sin and instituted the mass as an oblation for daily mortal and venial offences." Similar—but not precisely the same—views are ascribed by Vasquez to Ambrose Catharinus, and denounced by Latimer (Serm. iv. ed. Parker Soc., vol. i. p. 36); and Bishop Gardiner in 1548 says: "When men added to the mass an opinion of satisfaction and of a new redemption, they put it to another use than it was ordained for" (Dixon *Hist. of the Ch. of E.* iii. p. 264).

NOTE 14, see p. 181.

Some later Roman teaching on the sacrifice of the altar.

For the view referred to above the following references may be given—De Lugo *de veritate sacramenti eucharistiæ,* disp. xix. 5 (Lyons, 1636) : " Corpus Christi . . . destruitur humano modo, quatenus accipit *statum decliviorem* et talem quo reddatur inutile ad usus humanos corporis humani et aptum ad alios diversos usus per modum cibi : quare humano modo idem est ac si fieret verus panis et aptaretur ac condiretur in cibum, quæ mutatio sufficiens est ad verum sacrificium : fieri enim comestibile illud quod non erat comestibile et ita fieri comestibile ut jam non sit utile ad alios usus nisi per modum cibi major mutatio est quam aliæ quæ ex communi hominum mente sufficiebant ad verum sacrificium." Franzelin *tract. de ss. eucharistiæ sacramento et sacrificio,* p. 380 (Rome, 1868) : " Dat se ipsum ecclesiæ suae per suos ministros sacerdotes constituendum corpore et sanguine suo in tali existendi modo sub speciebus panis ac vini ut vere sit in statu cibi ac potus : ut (formaliter quatenus constituitur sub his speciebus) desinat omnis actus connaturalis vitæ corporeae pendens a sensibus: ut nihil secundum corpus possit agere connaturaliter: ut corpus ejus ac sanguis in quantum præsentia ejus alligatur speciebus permittatur quodammodo arbitrio creaturarum, ac si esset res inanimata. . . . Atqui talis 'exinanitio' . . . non solum satis intelligitur ut vere et proprie sacrificalis, sed etiam excepto sacrificio cruento in cruce nullam sublimiorem ac profundiorem rationem veri et proprii sacrificii concipere possumus." To support the phrase "exinanitio" Franzelin appeals only to a passage in certain *Responsiones ad Paulum Samos.* (ap. Labbe. *Concil.* i. 896) wrongly attributed to Dionysius Alex., where Phil. ii. 7 is interpreted of our Lord's condescension to us in communion. *Cf.* Einig, *tract. de ss. eucharistiæ mysterio* (Trèves, 1888), pp. 132—7. This little book is very useful for understanding the later Roman theory.

NOTE 15, see p. 187.

The "glorious interchanges" of the eucharist.

Some specimens of this language may be quoted from collects of the Leonine Sacramentary. See *P. L.* lv. 29, 148.

"Exercentes, Domine, gloriosa commercia offerimus quae dedisti ut te ipsum mereamur accipere."

"Altaribus tuis, Domine, munera terrena gratanter offerimus ut caelestia consequamur; damus terrena ut sumamus aeterna."

Note 16, see p. 197.

Presence at the eucharist of non-communicants.

Chrysostom, as is well known, condemns the practice of persons coming to the eucharist and not communicating: see *ad Ephes. hom.* iii. 4, 5 (*P. G.* lxii. 29 f.). But he would have admitted it in the case of the *consistentes*—*i.e.* those in the last stage of ecclesiastical penance. And while declining to admit to communion some monks banished from Alexandria, "till their case had been judicially decided," he allowed them "to partake in the prayers," *i.e.*, to be present at the eucharist: see Socrat. *H. E.* vi. 9. Chrysostom's words, moreover, are not the only ones bearing on the subject. Thus Tertullian, at the beginning of the third century, considers the case of those who would not come to the eucharist—"the prayers of the sacrifices "—on station (fast) days, because receiving the Lord's body would put an end to their station. He however would have them on these days stand at the altar as usual for the prayers of the eucharist and receive the Lord's body into their hands, reserving it for subsequent communion at home. "Thus by receiving and reserving the Lord's body both ends are secured, the participation in the sacrifice and the fulfilment of your service" (*de orat.* 14). And Clement of Alexandria, about the same date, contemplates its being left to the conscience of the persons present at the eucharist to receive or not. "Some, after dividing the eucharist according to custom, lay it upon each individual among the people to receive his portion [or not]. For it is best left to conscience to determine reception or avoidance" (*Strom.* i. 1. 5). Later, Eusebius (of Alexandria? 5th or 6th century) takes the line opposed to Chrysostom's, and would have those not fit to receive "stay through the prayers" and not go out "before the dismissal." See *Dic. of Chr. Biog.* ii. 307; Scudamore *Notit. Euch.* p. 393. Before the beginning of the middle ages this had become the established usage.

NOTE 17, see pp. 198, 255.

Effect of the Epistle to the Hebrews upon eucharistic doctrine in Ambrose and Chrysostom.

The effect of the Epistle to the Hebrews upon the fathers in forcing them to view the eucharistic worship and sacrifice upon the background of Christ's continual intercession and presentation of Himself in heaven, and not upon the background of the cross, is very marked. Thus St. Ambrose in the West (*in Psalm* xxxviii. 25, and *de offic.* i. 248), commenting on Hebr. x. 1, says — " The *shadow* was in the law; the *image* (*i.e.*, the reality under a veil) is in the Gospel; the truth (*i.e.* the unveiled reality) in the heavenly places." Then, in the first passage, he continues—"We have seen the chief of the priests coming to us; we have seen and heard Him offering for us His own blood: we priests follow as we may to offer sacrifice for the people, though weak in desert yet honourable in sacrifice. Because although Christ is not now seen to offer, yet He is Himself offered on earth when His body is offered: or rather He is Himself manifested as offering among us, it being His own word which sanctifies the sacrifice which is offered. He Himself stands by us, our advocate with the Father; nevertheless, we see Him not now: then we shall see Him when the image shall have passed and the truth come." Plainly the unseen reality of the eucharist is Christ *as He is in heaven*. So in the second passage. "Of old a lamb or a bullock was the offering, now Christ is offered; offered, that is, as man, as if accepting suffering: and He offers Himself as priest, that He may forgive our sins: here in image, there in truth, where with the Father He presents Himself for us as our advocate."

And St. Chrysostom, among Greeks, has noble passages to the same effect: see *in Hebr. hom.* xiv. 1, 2; *cf. Hom.* xvi. 2 (*P. G.* lxiii. 111, 112, 125). His point is to identify "spiritual" as applied to the church's worship with "heavenly." It is celebrated in a mystery on earth, but in fact all is heavenly or " in heaven "—priest and altar and all. Indeed "the church is heavenly: yea, it is nothing else than heavenly." Commenting on "the shadow of heavenly things" (Hebr. viii. 5), he says " What things does he call heavenly? The spiritual things which, though they are celebrated upon earth, are yet worthy of heaven. For when our Lord Jesus Christ lies 'slain' (Rev. v. 6), when the Spirit comes, when He who sits at the right hand of the Father is here . . . are not all these things heavenly?"

NOTE 18, see p. 262.

The four N. T. accounts of the institution.

I do not attempt to deal in this book with a tendency among some recent critics to deny that our Lord at the Last Supper really instituted the solemn commemoration of His death, and the communion in His body and blood. This is a matter which belongs to the general discussion of the historical character of the Gospels, and the trustworthiness of St. Paul's witness. I must content myself with referring to Dr. Sanday, in Hastings *Dic. of the Bible*, vol. ii. p. 638.

Assuming, however, the historical value of our records, it will be convenient to have the four accounts beside one another for purposes of comparison.

The words in the third column which are enclosed in brackets are not contained in some ancient authorities, and their right to stand in St. Luke's text is not quite certain.

APPENDED NOTES. 311

St. Mark	St. Matthew	St. Luke	St. Paul
		And he said unto them, With desire I have desired to eat this passover with you before I suffer: for I say unto you, I will not eat it, until it be fulfilled in the kingdom of God. And he received a cup, and when he had given thanks, he said, Take this, and divide it among yourselves: for I say unto you, I will not drink from henceforth of the fruit of the vine until the kingdom of God shall come.	For I received of the Lord that which also I delivered unto you, how that the Lord Jesus in the night in which he was betrayed
And as they were eating, he took bread, and when he had blessed, he brake it, and gave to them, and said, Take ye: this is my body. And he took a cup, and when he had given thanks, he gave to them, and they all drank of it. And he said unto them, This is my blood of the covenant, which is shed for many, Verily I say unto you, I will no more drink of the fruit of the vine, until that day when I drink it new in the kingdom of God.	And as they were eating, Jesus took bread, and blessed, and brake it; and he gave it to the disciples, and said, Take, eat, This is my body. And he took a cup, and gave thanks, and gave to them, saying, Drink ye all of it; for this is my blood of the covenant, which is shed for many unto remission of sins. But I say unto you, I will not drink henceforth of the fruit of the vine, until that day when I drink it new with you in my Father's kingdom.	And he took bread, and when he had given thanks, he brake it, and gave to them, saying, This is my body, [which is given for you: this do in remembrance of me. And the cup in like manner after supper, saying, This cup is the new covenant in my blood, even that which is poured out for you].	took bread: and when he had given thanks, he brake it, and said, This is my body which is for you: this do in remembrance of me. In like manner also the cup after supper, saying, This cup is the new covenant in my blood: this do, as oft as ye drink it, in remembrance of me.

NOTE 19, see p. 264.

The eucharist before the passion and after.

The whole argument of this book assumes that the eucharist is a communion in the spiritual body of the risen and living Christ; and therefore that it could only be rightly celebrated in the power of the Spirit, which was not given before Christ was glorified. How then could it be instituted before the passion? How could Christ, while yet in His mortal body, give His disciples His flesh and blood to eat and drink? To this question there is, I think, no answer, except by regarding the institution of the eucharist as an anticipation of glory akin to the Transfiguration. It is a natural interpretation of the Transfiguration to see in it an evidence that the glory already belonged to Christ's person, but was deliberately being suppressed that He might suffer and die. In any case it was an anticipation of the state of glory, and the institution of the eucharist was a like anticipation; just as, on the other hand, the eating and drinking after the resurrection was a (perhaps miraculous) reversion to the conditions of mortality.

NOTE 20, see p. 268.

On the sacrificial meaning of ποιεῖν and ἀνάμνησις.

I.

The same Hebrew word *'asah* means "to do," and, in a special sense, "to offer in sacrifice."

See Driver on Deut. xii. 27. "*Offer*] lit. *do* in a sacrificial sense, as often in P. (the "priestly document" of the Hexateuch), and occasionally besides." Thus the Greek word ποιεῖν bears in the LXX. the same sacrificial meaning, almost always as a translation of the Hebrew word, like ῥέζειν in classical authors and *facere* in Latin. This is habitual and indisputable. For instance, in Exod. xxix. 38 f., "Now this is that which thou shalt *offer* upon the altar: two lambs, etc. The one lamb thou shalt *offer* in the morning; and the other lamb thou shalt *offer* at even"—the word in the Greek for offer is ποιεῖν. So it is in Leviticus ix. 7, "*Offer* the sin-offering . . . *offer* the oblation of the people." So where in 1 Kings xi. 33, we read "They have *worshipped* Ashtoreth" (from the Hebrew *shachah*) it is in Greek ἐποίησε τῇ Ἀστάρτῃ. So in 2 Kings xvii. 32, ἐποίησαν ἑαυτοῖς ἐν οἴκῳ τῶν ὑψηλῶν stands for "they sacrificed for themselves in the high places." (See Gesenius, s.v. 'Asah.) Of this use of ποιεῖν there are from sixty to eighty instances in the LXX., and it is used of meal offerings as well as of animal sacrifices.

Does this use extend into the New Testament? It may be found in St. Luke ii. 27, τοῦ ποιῆσαι αὐτοὺς κατὰ τὸ εἰθισμένον τοῦ νόμου περὶ αὐτοῦ—"that they might offer according to the custom of the law on his behalf": for if ποιῆσαι merely means "to do" it would naturally have been followed immediately by περὶ αὐτοῦ. And in the passages about the institution of the eucharist where the word occurs (1 Cor. xi. 24, 25, Luke xxii. 19), if we translate "offer," the construction of the sentence becomes more easy. (See Mason *Faith of the Gospel*, p. 309.) Thus τοῦτό μού ἐστιν τὸ σῶμα ... τοῦτο ποιεῖτε ... τοῦτο τὸ ποτήριον ... τοῦτο ποιεῖτε is certainly a more natural sentence if τοῦτο throughout has the same meaning—"This is my body (blood); this offer," instead of "This is my body (blood); do this (action)." And in the case of the following words, τοῦτο ποιεῖτε, ὁσάκις ἐὰν πίνητε, it is awkward to translate "Do this as often as ye drink (absolutely)"; or "Do this action, as often as ye drink (the cup)." The sentence runs more easily if we translate "offer this (cup of wine) as often as ye drink it."

The weak point, however, in this argument is the fact that this sense of ποιεῖν is very rarely recognized in the literature of the early church. Certainly Justin (*dial. c. Tryph.* 41) so interprets the word in the institution of the eucharist. The offering of the fine flour, he says, was a type of the bread of the eucharist "which Christ Jesus gave to us to offer," τοῦ ἀρτοῦ τῆς εὐχαριστίας ὃν ... Ι. Χ. παρέδωκε ποιεῖν. He makes the object of the verb to be the bread and not the action. And this is repeated later, c. 70. Also in the Byzantine Liturgy there is one use of the word in this sense (Brightman, *op. cit.*, p. 362): καιρὸς τοῦ ποιῆσαι τῷ κυρίῳ. Otherwise it does not appear to be recognized. Harnack thinks that the "Gentile Christians might suppose that they had to understand ποιεῖν in the sense of θύειν" (see *Hist. of Dogm.* Eng. trans. i. p. 209, n. ²), but I know no grounds for this opinion.

On the whole, then, there is not sufficient evidence to entitle us to say that ποιεῖν bears the sacrificial sense in the New Testament.

II.

The matter stands similarly with ἀνάμνησις. Μνημόσυνον is the regular word for a sacrificial memorial before God in the LXX. (*cf.* Acts x. 4), but on two occasions ἀνάμνησις is used in the text of the canonical books, and both times in this sense: Lev. xxiv. 7, "They (the shew bread) shall be for loaves for a memorial lying before the Lord"; and Numb. x. 10: The blowing of the trumpets "shall be a memorial for you before your God." Besides this it is used in the titles of Psalms xxxvii. and lxix., probably in a similar sense. But in Wisdom xvi. 6 it is used for a reminder to men, and in Heb. x. 3 the use is ambiguous.

In the phrase τοῦτο ποιεῖτε εἰς τὴν ἐμὴν ἀνάμνησιν the sense of "memorial before God" is quite in place, but the weak point again in the case of those who maintain it, is the fact that it was not apparently so understood by the Christian church. The phrase of the anaphora, "Therefore we remembering Thy blessed passion," etc. (μεμνημένοι οὖν), implies that they understood our

Lord's words to mean, "This do to remember Me." And this phrase probably goes back to very early times.

NOTE 21, see pp. 41, 288.

The social aspect of the sacraments.[1]

The phrase "Extra ecclesiam nulla salus" ("outside the church no salvation"), has been taken as the very badge of an intolerant and narrow churchmanship. Yet I cannot but think that recent study of the earliest Christian literature is bringing us back to recognize how very large a measure of truth it expresses. This result has been partly due to the direct or indirect influence of Albrecht Ritschl, both in Germany and in England. He perceived afresh that the visible community was of the essence of Christianity from the first, and that it was through membership in the Christian commonwealth that men were to find their salvation. In other words, if by "the salvation" we mean that state in which the redeemed abide under the shelter of the divine covenant in Christ, then the books of our New Testament would lead us to believe that the only subject of the salvation is the community—that the new covenant, as truly as the old, is a covenant with a people and with individuals only as members of the people. Therefore "extra ecclesiam

[1] This note is substantially a reprint of an article contributed to the *Pilot* of March 3rd, 1900.

nulla salus," if by "salus" we mean the security of the covenant.

The recent recognition of this truth in Protestant circles in England is likely in the long run to lead to important results. Thus the recent repudiation by the editor of "The Evangelical Free Church Catechism" of the idea of the invisible church as being an " invention of the sixteenth century," and the emphasis laid by both the catechism and its editor on membership in the one visible catholic church—even if from our point of view the unity of the church is somewhat inadequately conceived—may well mark an epoch in English religion.

But there is little use in bringing it about that the important function of the church should be recognized again in the original purpose of Christ and in the teaching of His apostles, unless it is also brought home in its positive meaning to the contemporary conscience; and unless we can obviate the plain moral objections which are felt to any proposal to identify fellowship with Christ with membership in any particular community or set of communities. The fundamental moral conscience in us—which is the only secure ground on which any positive religious belief can be based—imperatively demands that no one who is morally sound in heart and will should be regarded as outside the approval of Christ. Yet multitudes of good men are, and have been, outside the church, however freely the church be conceived, so long as it be taken to mean anything visible at all.

Now on this point we are practically all agreed. There is hardly a thoughtful Christian of any denomination, however strict in orthodoxy, who could bring himself to doubt, under any pressure of external authority, that a sincerely good man— a man really following the best light he has got —was certain of the approval of God and of ultimate fellowship in the kingdom of Christ. Here then we are all agreed. Yet in popular estimation it is just this fundamental moral principle which conflicts with any exclusive spiritual claim made on behalf of the visible church. What, therefore, we have got to make good men see is that—though we cannot judge one another before the time, and are bound to believe that to follow the light is to be finding Christ; though again the church of the new covenant has plainly, like the church of the old, fallen so far short of its ideal as to have given men at times no slight excuse for identifying it rather with Babylon, or with the State, than with the City of God—yet still, after the largest acknowledgments have been made under these heads, the intention of Christ remains clear—to found one visible society as the sphere of His covenant of love; and the obligation therefore upon loyal disciples to seek to realize this intention is still paramount; and its moral meaning is still perspicuous.

For its moral meaning is to declare that there is no divine fellowship except in human brotherhood; it is to refuse to separate acceptableness with God from the actual service of man. This is the moral meaning of saying—your salvation shall lie in the life of a community. Our Lord, the great Master of human life, chose to test men's religious seriousness by their willingness to endure the discipline involved in membership in a body which both acknowledged a lofty moral and social standard, and also, because it was catholic, required its members to "receive" into actual fellowship men and women of all sorts.

We easily see how very real a discipline in patience and forbearance is involved in the idea of a catholic society. A catholic must be a tolerant, large-hearted person. If the original Jewish disciples found it sorely hard to tolerate the Gentiles in equal fellowship; if the Gentile Christians at Rome a little later were disposed to be intolerant of Jewish scruples; if it put a strain upon the masters to welcome their slaves into the brotherhood — these were but examples of the severe discipline which was to be laid on men all down the ages by membership in a catholic body. Of course, the church may in practice so lower her moral and social standard, and may grow so acquiescent in the divisions of Christendom, as effectually to annul both forms of moral discipline. When you have got a different communion for each nation and class, and a lax moral requirement in all alike, membership in the Christian church has, no doubt, so far ceased to involve any moral effort, and ceased accordingly to have any moral value. But the intention of Christ abides, and its moral meaning abides. His faithful servants will continually recur in heart and intellect, with profound penitence and prayer, to their Master's intention of the One Body and the moral meaning which it is meant to carry.

My object in writing this is to urge all those who are interested in the course of Christian thought to recognize that merely to proclaim as a dogma the obligation of the church and the sin of schism will have no effect at all—grounded though the proclamation be securely enough on the books of the New Testament—unless the moral meaning of the church, the moral and social meaning of the catholic brotherhood, is brought home to people's hearts simultaneously or antecedently. And it is of the greatest importance to apply this general principle to the particular subject-matter of the sacraments. Church and sacraments are intimately and necessarily bound up together. There is a great deal—perhaps a disproportionate amount—of teaching about the sacraments being given in many of our Anglican pulpits to-day. They are enforced from the side of authority. They are enforced as means of grace to help the individual life. Their adaptation to our two-fold nature—material as well as spiritual—is ably and truly set out. But I cannot but think that their moral appeal to what is best in men would be made infinitely greater if their connection with the church as an organized brotherhood, if their

APPENDED NOTES.

obvious social bearing, were both better appreciated and more dwelt upon.

For, in fact, if we consider them one by one we shall perceive easily enough how exceedingly important a part of their meaning and efficacy lies in the fact that they are ceremonies of a society.

1. This is conspicuously true of baptism, which as a sacrament of initiation was taken over from the Jewish church. The child of Jewish parents was *born* a Jew. He required no second birth, but only obedience, beginning with circumcision, to the law of the covenant to which he already belonged.[1] But the Gentile who desired fellowship with the people of God was—certainly before our Lord's time—initiated by a series of ceremonies of which the most universal was a baptism of purification; the most universal because, of the ceremonies which accompanied it, circumcision only applied to men, and the sacrifice was only possible at Jerusalem while the temple stood. This ceremonial initiation was characterized as a "new birth." The proselyte was born again; that is to say, he was to forget his own people and his father's house and make a fresh start on a new tradition, with a new faith, and a changed set of

---

[1] Thus the Christian counterpart of the painful rite of circumcision is, strictly speaking, not baptism, which corresponds to birth in a Jew, but self-denial or mortification. In Genesis xvii. 14, the uncircumcised male is to be cut off because he has *broken* the covenant.

social customs and duties. He was a new man because he was a member of a new society.[1] When Nicodemus expresses his difficulty at the idea of an old man re-born, as suggested by our Lord, it is at least probable that by introducing the thought of initiation into the kingdom by baptism, by being born of water, our Lord intends in part to meet his difficulty.[2] At any rate, it is a certain fact, as Schürer and Edersheim prove to us, that the baptism of a proselyte was a necessary part of his new birth as a Jew. Now Christian baptism—of "the Spirit" as well as "of water"—is a far deeper thing, and involves a far deeper change in the basis of the personal life, than Jewish baptism, which was only a social change. But the idea of regeneration is far more intelligible if its social bearing is still kept prominent; and that Christian baptism was as early and as necessarily thought of as being baptism into the body, as it was as baptism into Christ, appears in St. Paul's phrase: "By one Spirit were we all baptized into one body." It appears also in the fact that Christianity took over from Judaism, and very likely from the first, the institution of sponsors—the baptismal witnesses of the Talmud; an institution which is meant to emphasize the acceptance of the newly-baptized into a society and the

[1] See on the baptism of Jewish proselytes Schürer *Jewish People*, Div. ii. Vol. ii. pp. 319 ff. nd Edersheim's *Life and Times of Jesus the Messiah*, Vol. ii., app. xii.

[2] John iii. 3—5.

obligation of the society for the education of its members. In fact, the more we realize the social bearing of baptism the more reasonably we shall value the practice of infant baptism, but also the more emphatically shall we insist on again giving prominence and reality to the institution of sponsors.

2. Baptism puts at our disposal new spiritual power for our personal life, but it does this because it incorporates us into a new society. And the new "member," thus incorporated, proceeds either at once, or, in the case of an infant, as his powers mature, to receive his full citizenship in the New Jerusalem by his " sealing " in confirmation. This laying on of hands again conveys an individual endowment—it is the strengthening of the individual life by the gift of the Holy Ghost. But it is also a social ceremony with a social meaning. It is outwardly a benediction from the chief officer of the society, and it conveys to the confirmed his full right in the royal and priestly body. From very early days it was accompanied by anointing: it was at least called an " unction " from St. John's days. This meant, what the early mediæval ritualists expressly stated, that the member on whom hands were laid was being consecrated king and priest—consecrated, that is, to his full civic and religious rights.[1] This primitive

[1] *Cf.* quotations in *The Church and the Ministry* (Longmans), ed. 4, p. 82.

idea makes thoroughly reasonable the novel ceremony of our present Anglican rite, which associates with confirmation the formal acceptance by the now responsible individual of the moral duties of his Christian position. But we have lamentably let slip the accompanying idea of the lay priesthood and citizenship, an idea so essential to that reform of the church on really representative lines which is so widely desired, and for which confirmation ought to afford so significant a basis.

3. The now fully-initiated churchman continually renews and intensifies in the eucharist this new life, which is the divine and human life of Jesus communicated to him—His "flesh" and "blood"—and which for this very reason is also the cementing and deepening of the social cohesion of the brotherhood. The root of the Semitic tradition of sacrifice lies in the idea of a divine life sacramentally communicated by the God who is worshipped to the tribe, or society of some sort, which worships Him, and which is His own people, in some special relation of covenant with Him. It is this fundamental human instinct of sacrifice which the eucharist expresses anew in a perfect form. It binds those who share it to one another in binding them to God. It is a "communion" —a common sharing. The intimate association, at the beginning, of the holy sacrament of Christ's body and blood with the fraternal meal, which at first preceded it and afterwards followed it at a

later hour, of course kept intensely alive its social meaning. It was the sacrament of fraternity. "Because the bread is one, we, the many, are one body," wrote St. Paul. And others by a different road reach the same conception: "As this bread was once scattered upon the mountains, and, having been gathered together became one, so let Thy church be gathered together from the ends of the earth into Thy kingdom."[1] "By which very sacrament (of the bread) our people is exhibited as made one; so that as many grains collected into one and ground together and mingled make one loaf, so in Christ, who is the heavenly loaf (bread), we should hold that there is one body to which our company is joined and united."[2] "For as this bread was scattered upon the mountains, and having been gathered together became one, so also, O Lord, gather together Thy holy church from every race and every country and city and village and household, and make it a living catholic church."[3]

St. Augustine realized, as hardly any one else, the meaning of the catholic church as the embodiment of "love as wide as the world"; and he abominated the sin of schism as being the violation of love and tolerant fellowship by narrowness, pride and selfishness. We should expect him,

---

[1] *Didache* ix. 4. [2] Cyprian *ep.* 73, 13.
[3] Bishop Serapion's Prayer of the Oblation, in his newly discovered liturgy; also *Ap. Const.* vii. 25.

therefore, to realize pre-eminently the social bearings of the eucharist; and, indeed, he does so—not least in connection with the eucharistic sacrifice. The very spirit and essence of St. Augustine's teaching about the eucharistic sacrifice is what we find in the two post-communion prayers—would that they were not merely alternative prayers!—of our Communion Service; for, according to Augustine, the chief point about the eucharist is that therein the church offers *herself* through Christ, as His body, to the Father—the body identifying itself with the sacrifice of the head, and realizing in her "holy fellowship" the identity of spirit which binds her to Christ.

4. The normal sacraments, which alone as "generally necessary for salvation" were in the age of Rabanus Maurus reckoned "the sacraments of the church," were baptism, confirmation, and the eucharist. But there were other sacred rites of spiritual efficacy suited to a more or less abnormal need, or to states of life which, however common, were special, and these too, had been, or came to be, reckoned sacraments; and their significance also was largely social. Thus—to say nothing of marriage, the social significance of which cannot fall out of sight—from the first Christians were liable to fall into sins so grave as to be "unto death": the moral equivalents, that is, of those sins for which, under the old covenant, there was no atoning sacrifice but the penalty of death. These involved excommunication, which

was, especially at first, a social act—a judgment on an offender by the whole community acting as a body through its officers; and the excommunicated member was subjected to a punishment or penance which tested the sincerity of his penitence; and, when his penitence was approved, he was readmitted to communion or absolved, again by the society acting through its officers. The history of this institution of ecclesiastical penance must be traced elsewhere. Here it is only necessary to point out that it is in its very essence a social judgment. Sin is not only sin against God. It is also an offence against the life of the community. The community is to judge it and punish it, and then absolve from it by readmitting the offender into the common life. It is often said that ecclesiastical absolution is either a "charm," *i.e.* an arbitrary power committed to a priest apart from moral conditions; or a mere declaration of what is in any case true, that God forgives a penitent person. But this is no true dilemma. Absolution (or its refusal) is a moral *judgment* passed by the society through its officer upon an offender. The point is that Christ has attached to the judgment by the society, of condemnation or acquittal, so divine a sanction and meaning, as to make it evident to us that He willed our fellowship with Himself to be normally dependent upon our admitted fellowship in the body. This principle inheres in "the sacrament of penance" and ecclesiastical absolution, however administered.

It is always administered more or less amiss except where this principle is kept in distinct view. And it must never be forgotten how prominent among the objects of our reformers was the restoration of the old corporate discipline. The directions of the Prayer Book for dealing with the individual penitent, whose sins lie heavy upon his private conscience, can only be rightly viewed upon the background of the public discipline which it was sought to restore.

5. Finally we come to Holy Orders. Raymund of Sabunde, the fifteenth century schoolman, gives us the true point of view for estimating the apostolic succession in the ministry when he says: "Because the spiritual life consists in love and unity, therefore it was most suitable that it should be ordained that men should, in Christ's stead, administer the sacrament of salvation to men, in order that their mutual unity might thus be provided for."[1] The cohesion of the body, that is to say, was secured by providing a succession of persons down the ages who should be authorized stewards of the divine gifts for man's salvation; because, by the necessity laid upon men to look for these gifts at the hands of certain authorized stewards, their tendency to follow merely private inclinations into separation would be counteracted and checked. The official ministry was thus to be in each community a centre of unity, and by the mutual

[1] *Theol. Naturalis*, tit. 303.

cohesion of these officers of the churches the unity of the whole catholic body was to be secured. The church must needs have had its officers who would be representatives of the people; but the necessity that they should also derive their authority in due succession from those who had gone before them, was to provide a backbone of continuity for each church, and for the church as a whole, which should be capable of resisting the centrifugal tendencies of the individual and the congregation.

Now these ideas with regard to the sacraments are indisputably catholic. They are the ideas of the undivided church. But if this is so, there is surely grave need that they should be more considered than they are at present by those of us who are most keenly sacramentalist. It is not only within the area of Protestantism that an over-individualistic way of thinking about religion has prevailed. It prevailed also in the unreformed theology of the Reformation period and the subsequent epoch. There, too, the tendency was to regard the salvation of the individual as the main, or almost sole, object of religion. The same tendency dominated the revival of the sacramental teaching in the Tractarian movement. But that movement restored to us the idea of the church. And what we now need is to let our thought of the church and of the sacraments recover its original social colouring, so that we may restore the conception of human brotherhood to its true and dominant place among Christian conceptions. For indeed the best modern conscience is to be reached and touched and won in no way so effectively as by a strong and consistent appeal to the principle of brotherhood.

www.ingramcontent.com/pod-product-compliance
Lightning Source LLC
Chambersburg PA
CBHW050836230426
43667CB00012B/2017